MERCEDES-BENZ

MACMILLAN

O_2

NOTCUTTS

EASYJET

AVIVA

MCDONALD'S

JOHN LEWIS

SAINSBURY'S

MINI

GALAXY

BURTON'S BISCUITS

PWC

AMVBBDO

MCLAREN

JACK DANIEL'S

BT SPORT

HAILO

THE FAMOUS GROUSE

AXE

FOSTER'S

BRITISH AIRWAYS

NATIONAL LOTTERY

JAGUAR

UNILEVER

FAIRTRADE FOUNDATION

BRITISH GAS

CHANNEL 4

PADDY POWER

DEPAUL

First published in Great Britain and the United States in 2015 by Kogan Page Limited.

2nd Floor	1518 Walnut Street	4737/23 Ansari Road
45 Gee Street	Suite 1100	Daryaganj
London EC1V 3RS	Philadelphia PA 19102	New Delhi 110002
United Kingdom	USA	India

www.koganpage.com

© The Marketing Society, 2015
The right of Hugh Burkitt to be identified as the author of this work has been asserted by him in accordance with the Copyright, Designs and Patents Act 1988.

ISBN   978 0 7494 7378 5
E-ISBN 978 0 7494 7379 2

British Library Cataloguing-in-Publication Data
A CIP record for this book is available from the British Library.

Library of Congress Cataloging-in-Publication Data

CIP data is available.
Library of Congress Control Number: 2014037440

Typeset by So Design Consultants, Bristol, UK
Printed and bound in Great Britain by Henry Ling Limited, Dorchester, Dorset

MARKETING EXCELLENCE 3

Award-winning companies reveal
the secrets of their success

KoganPage

LONDON PHILADELPHIA NEW DELHI

CONTENTS

FOREWORD
By Martin Glenn
President of The Marketing Society

When I was asked to write the Foreword for the first edition of Marketing Excellence in 2006, I spent some time agonising about what exactly 'Marketing Excellence' is.

My definition had three elements:
- Outperforming our competitors.
- Sustaining this performance over time.
- Achieving consistently high standards of performance, which is more important than striving for perfection.

Nearly a decade later, these observations still seem to me to hold good, and my own less than perfect record as a marketer has not discouraged The Marketing Society from inviting me to become their President.

As President, I have been keen to encourage marketers to take a more commercial approach to business, and to develop their leadership skills so that they are ready to take on the chief executive role. Too many businesses in the UK are currently run by accountants.

Accountants count the money but it is marketers who must make it. And as marketers we must never stop learning. These thirty case histories provide a wonderful series of lessons in how to excel, and I would urge marketers at all stages of their career to study them.

Martin Glenn
President of The Marketing Society
Chief Executive, United Biscuits

THANKS

Our thanks go first to all the companies and agencies who have allowed us to publish their success stories. While we have used the original award submissions as the basis for these case studies, we have reworked, edited, and in some cases updated them to make this book as valuable as possible to the reader.

The Marketing Society's associate partner for more than a decade has been *Marketing* magazine and we would particularly like to thank all the team at Haymarket who have helped us build the scope and stature of the Awards – especially Claire Beale, Helen Horton, Lisa Lione and Steven Lewis. We are also enormously grateful for the financial support during the past four years of BT, Unilever, SapientNitro and Yahoo; and for the contribution to the design of our awards by Tangible and, most recently, 18 Feet & Rising.

Laura Mazur of Writers4Management has done a brilliant job in persuading the entrants to part with their material, chasing up the illustrations and editing the final manuscript in a timely and thoughtful manner. Ann Gould of 26 Marketing has kept us all to schedule. Thanks also to Gemma Greaves, Sarah Woodley and Sharon Conway at The Marketing Society for all their valued input.

The original 'editors' of this book are, of course, the judges who choose the winners in each year. We are very grateful to all of them for the time they have given during the awards process, and especially so to those who have added their wise comments at the beginning of each chapter. We would also like to thank all those who have entered The Marketing Society Awards in the past four years. There have been many excellent cases written, which we have not had space to include. Without these entries there would have been no competition.

Finally, our thanks, in anticipation, to our readers. If you can draw lessons from these cases that help you develop your own marketing success story, then you will be helping us prove that marketing excellence is indeed the key driver of business growth.

Too many businesses in the UK are currently run by accountants. Accountants count the money but it is marketers who must make it.

Martin Glenn,
President, The Marketing Society

INTRODUCTION
By Hugh Burkitt
Chief Executive, The Marketing Society

This latest collection of thirty success stories from the past four years of
The Marketing Society Excellence Awards brings us neatly up to our thirtieth
anniversary in 2015.

Back in 1985 there was no requirement for the winners to labour over a carefully
crafted 2000 word submission. The great and the good of The Marketing Society got
together and picked out their own favourites from the UK market place.

The first consumer award winner was International Distillers & Vintners – now
part of Diageo – for Smirnoff, which is still the market leader in vodka. Among the
runners-up was Channel 4, another brand which has stood the test of time – winning
our Grand Prix with Sainsbury's for their work on the Paralympics just two years ago.

In the past decade Sainsbury's overall performance in our Awards has been
outstanding with eight winning papers, four highly commended and a Marketer
of the Year – Sarah Warby. Only John Lewis has come close with five wins and also
a Marketer of the Year – Craig Inglis. These two outstanding retailers have also
slugged it out on television at Christmas in a battle to win the hearts and wallets
of the nation and here you can study both their very different routes to success.

Sainsbury's and John Lewis' success would not be possible without the continuing
delivery of an excellent shopping experience both in store and online, and reflecting
on the general lessons of the stories in this book I am struck by the importance of the
product or service that underpins every brand.

In this volume there are four good examples of famous brands that have improved their
market position by improving their product. easyJet revamped their whole marketing
mix in the past four years under the leadership of Carolyn McCall and Peter Duffy, and
at the heart of their success there has been a radical improvement in their customer
service, which has earned them dramatic gains in sales, profits and share price.

BT added a completely new benefit to their brand with the introduction of BT Sport and transformed the reputation of the parent brand in the process, Jaguar have raised the reputation of their marque with the launch of the F-Type, and British Airways has re-established itself as the nation's favourite airline by re-connecting with its staff through its "To fly. To serve." campaign.

British Airways also benefited from being sponsors of the London 2012 Olympics, as did McDonald's who won our communication category last year by overcoming initial criticism of their involvement and celebrating the general public's role in this national triumph. Sponsoring the Olympics is an expensive activity but there is also a good selection of stories here from brands with more ambition than cash.

Depaul, the charity for destitute young people, neatly connected homelessness and moving house by starting a company that sells Depaul cardboard boxes to people with a home to move to.

Paddy Power, which has had its collar felt by the ASA on a couple of occasions recently, continued its cheeky approach to publicity in a very crowded market by producing a widely admired campaign in partnership with Stonewall against homophobia in football. Amongst other achievements they gained 320 million Twitter impressions for a total cost of less than half of Wayne Rooney's weekly pay. Notcutts Garden Centre also impressed our cost conscious Finance Directors panel by coming up with a loyalty scheme that customers thought was so good they eagerly paid to join.

Finally a word of congratulations to all the agencies listed in the Appendix, but especially to AMVBBDO who after years of writing successful papers on behalf of clients such as Sainsbury's, BT and Aviva have managed to appear in this edition as winners themselves of this year's Employee Engagement Award.

Hugh Burkitt
Chief Executive Officer
The Marketing Society

CHAPTER 1

01

Finding consumer insight

Finding those great customer insights that are the bedrock of successful marketing campaigns takes both hard work and lateral thinking.

Both these case studies illustrate this. Mercedes-Benz had to turn around its brand image with the core 35-to-54 target group by making the brand feel more sporty and dynamic. But, rather than follow traditional routes to gathering actionable insights, Mercedes-Benz used the modern science of biometrics to gauge actual physical responses to driving the cars. It showed the strong emotional and physical response provoked by the car's sound.

The subsequent multi-media campaign delivered the results by building on the insight that powerful sounds could trigger emotions such as excitement, happiness and nostalgia. A key element was to encourage users to create sound 'mash-ups' to share on social networks.

Insight was at the core of the campaign from Macmillan. It had set itself challenging and seemingly conflicting aims: create an urgency in people to donate but at the same time not let this appeal put off those it helped or prevent them from seeking help. It needed clearly-distinctive calls to action.

Vast amounts of clinical data, brand insights, focus groups, conversations with medical professionals, listening to calls and spending time online were analysed. The finding from the data, that you can feel so alone whether cancer affects you directly or indirectly, led to the powerful insight that 'no one should face cancer alone'. The results were dramatic: a 33% increase in revenues.

Robert Bridge
VP, Head of International Marketing
Yahoo

MERCEDES-BENZ
Enjoying the sound of brand success

SNAPSHOT
Mercedes-Benz took a lateral approach to insight-gathering by using biometric science to make the brand relevant to a key target market.

AGENCIES
AMVBBDO, Maxus, Weapon7, Holler

KEY INSIGHTS
- Mercedes-Benz had to confront a brand image among the important 35-54 year-old target audience that saw it languishing in terms of its sporty and dynamic credentials.
- The revelation that the sound of the exhaust was what really got hearts racing led to a multi-platform campaign centred around an engaging sensory experience.
- The power of that insight saw the brand beating both its rivals in terms of sales for the first time in many years.

SUMMARY
Mercedes-Benz is a world-famous automotive brand, part of the German-based group Daimler. It was facing a challenge in the UK with its E-Class range, one of its oldest model brands and a critical bridge between a new range of small, dynamic cars at one end and large high-end luxury limousines at the other. Even with the launch of a new E-Class model, the brand images of the two other key competitors in the class, Audi and BMW, were rated as more desirable by the target audience of 35-54 year olds.

The company needed to get that group to think again about the E-Class to give sales a boost. In-depth research found that among younger drivers characteristics such as 'sporty' and 'dynamic' resonated the most so the company decided to put the focus on the E63 AMG, the sportiest E-Class car.

Rather than follow traditional routes to gathering actionable insights, the brand team decided to employ the modern science of biometrics to gauge actual physical responses to driving the cars. This revealed that the sound of the car provoked a strong emotional and physical response, confirming its sporty credentials. The resulting interactive, multi-media campaign imaginatively exploited these findings to show how powerful sounds can trigger emotions such as excitement, happiness and nostalgia. A key element was encouraging users to create sound 'mash-ups' to share on social networks.

The results exceeded expectations. Brochure downloads increased by 117% and test drive requests by 80%. More significantly, sales went up by 38% compared to sector growth of only 9%.

BATTLING AGAINST BRAND IMAGE

Mercedes-Benz E-Class is the long-standing centre of gravity of the Mercedes-Benz brand. One of the oldest model brands, it represents a bridge between a new range of small, dynamic cars at one end and large high-end luxury limousines at the other. A brand new E-Class had been launched a year earlier (Figure 1) but, after an initial period of interest, it soon came under sales pressure once more. So the company set itself two challenging objectives:
• Make 35-54 year olds reappraise the Mercedes-Benz E-Class and increase the level of enquiries (requests for test drives and brochures) from this group.
• Drive a 10% increase in Mercedes-Benz E-Class new car sales, year-on-year.

Figure 1. Mercedes-Benz E-Class

This would not be easy. First, the new E-Class was going up against two of the most respected models in the world. Mercedes' rivals had come to dominate the sector in the battleground of 'medium-sized executive saloons'. Audi's A6 had garnered both plaudits and sales since the latest version was launched in 2011. Even more revered was BMW's 5 Series, widely regarded as the best four-door saloon ever produced.

As *AutoCar* magazine put it: "For 23 years, every iteration of the BMW 5 Series that has gone up against the Mercedes E-Class has come out on top." In other words, to succeed the brand would have to break with a pattern of defeat more than two decades old.

Secondly, it had to confront its image problem. The 5 Series and the A6 were not only seen as the pre-eminent cars but the manufacturers behind them, BMW and Audi, were both generally regarded by the target audience as comparatively more desirable brands. In their eyes, a Mercedes-Benz was a status car for 'the more mature driver'. As one Audi owner put it: "I wouldn't want to buy a badge that says: 'You've made it but you're putting the brakes on'".

So there was a problem at both the product and brand level in terms of facing superior competition. Admittedly, some inroads had been made into the problem over the last two years, but for the E-Class segment, the problem was particularly acute. The company and its agency needed to find a more radical solution.

WHAT MAKES THESE CAR BUYERS TICK

The starting point was to connect with BMW 5 Series and Audi A6 owners, inviting them to describe their cars. They responded with fondness and enthusiasm. That was followed by correlation analysis of brand consideration and brand perception in the prestige auto sector. Two discoveries were integral to the eventual creative solution.

1. Sporty credentials are fundamental.

The way that rival products and rival brands were fondly described was remarkably similar – descriptions that were subsequently confirmed by New Car Buyer Survey (NCBS) car characteristics tracking studies. Perception that a brand is driven by younger people, it turned out, is highly correlated with perceptions of the brand as being 'sporty' and 'dynamic'. So the decision was taken to showcase the sportiest E-Class model of all – the E63 AMG – to emphasise the sporty image of the class as a whole.

2. Physical experience is more important than design.

BMW 5 Series and Audi A6 owners tended to use descriptions of 'experience' as evidence of still being young(ish). Adventure holidays, extreme sports (though often not so extreme) and even risk-laden business deals were among the activities mentioned that got their pulses going.

As one respondent put it, these were things that meant "you're living, not just existing." It reminded the brand team of a quote from a colleague at AMG: "We develop the engine to prompt the release of large amounts of adrenaline". To put it another way, the experience of driving an AMG is specially engineered to elicit a physiological response in its driver.

However, while it had been engineered for a specific purpose, the big question to answer was whether it actually delivered on its promise. The answer was to measure what it really means to experience the E63 AMG. Historically, that would have been done by commissioning qualitative groups with drivers, but this time it was decided to take a lateral approach: use biometric science to understand the real, unbiased biological effects of driving the car.

READING THE RESPONSES

The team approached Hidalgo Ltd, the company that monitored Felix Baumgartner as he base-jumped from the edge of space. Together they devised a methodology to gauge the true physiological impact of driving an E63 AMG. Three male subjects aged between 29 and 50 were fitted with a life monitor, which was a unique piece of mobile technology designed to increase understanding of how the body is performing and adapting to different pressures, strains and environments, along with a Brainband EEG headset.

Each driver independently performed circuits of a private race track, with their biometric data viewed under acceleration and braking conditions. Each driver also had a complete set of biometric measures tracked, including: activity in the pleasure centre of the brain, heart rate variability, breathing waveforms, breathing rate, tri-axis accelerometry, temperature and galvanic skin response. The data was compared to Hidalgo's database.

An example of the results came from one driver aged 40:
- The instantaneous heart rate and heart rate variability showed a marked anticipatory response as did the galvanic skin response.
- The positive (excitement/exhilaration) response started approximately six seconds before beginning acceleration.

In fact, there was a reproducible physiological response among all three drivers that suggested extreme excitement. Of particular interest was an anticipatory heart rate and galvanic response in all three subjects when standing still, which began six seconds prior to motion. As Hidalgo stated in its analysis: "The finding of an anticipatory instantaneous heart rate response is both exciting and valuable to understand further. This is similar to the type of response seen in highly trained special operations soldiers prior to taking a shot at a target". (Dr. Ekta Sood, Hidalgo Limited, March 2013.)

This was so interesting because the key stimuli that caused the anticipatory response were primarily attributed to the sound the car emitted from its exhaust. It thus became apparent that sound could be used to elicit a physiological response (Figure 2). It meant that the team had uncovered a non-tactile sensory stimulus that had deep emotional resonance with drivers. Significantly, this was a sensory agent that could possibly be used to make people not only feel physically through interactive experiences, but remotely too through advertising.

Further investigation was necessary to understand this phenomenon with current performance car owners to discover what it was that made them so appealing and to gauge whether sound was as significant as the biometrics suggested. So 11 ethnographic in-depth studies were conducted among performance car owners (Mercedes-Benz, BMW and Audi), at home and out and about in their cars.

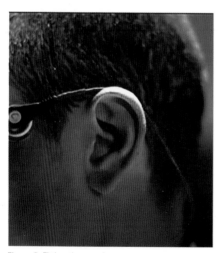

Figure 2. Fitting the ear piece

Within each session, their world was photographed and filmed throughout to provide a richer and deeper understanding of their lifestyle and priorities. What became immediately apparent was the universal appeal and significance of sound. Above all else, the sound of the exhaust note generated a highly-animated response from the respondents. It was the sound that created the emotional bond between driver and car. Not only that, the sound of the exhaust was a sensation they primarily used to signify a car as being an authentic performance car. It could provide the all-important sporty credentials.

MAKING A BIG NOISE

The Mercedes-Benz E63 AMG has an incredible sound, as became obvious through the biometric testing – the kind of sound that instantly provokes a strong emotional and physical response. The brief to the communications agency, AMVBBDO, was to demonstrate how these powerful sounds could trigger emotions – and for real. People had to feel the emotive power of sound first hand and to engage with it on the devices they were already using most regularly.

The interactive, multi-media campaign explored how sound has the power to incite a range of emotions, such as excitement, happiness and nostalgia. An interactive digital experience allowed users to build, layer upon layer, their own personal audio and video 'mash-up' using a range of sounds, all featuring the exhaust notes of the E63 AMG and other sonic elements.

The sound bites were specifically chosen for their ability to stimulate an emotional response in the observers. Once they had created their own 'mash-up' they were invited to share their creation on social networks, using *#soundwithpower*, for a chance to have their version air on TV during the second burst of the campaign.

The TV campaign drove the audience to the digital experience by demonstrating the human response to sound. The ad stood out by showing the real (not simulated) responses of one man to a variety of emotionally resonant sounds. The ad opened with a man being fitted with a suit and ear piece. He was then played various sounds, such as a baby's cry, crashing waves, a scene from a film, a favourite piece of music and the roar of the E63 AMG (Figures 3a to 3h).

Figures 3a to 3h. The TV campaign

As he heard each sound, the suit lit up in different ways, with his physical and neurological response to sound fed into built-in LED light panels. The television commercial directed the audience to the online 'mash-up' tool, hosted on the Mercedes-Benz website. Users were able to create their own audio-visual mash-ups directly in the browser whether on desktop, tablet or mobile. They were never more than a click away from a test drive or brochure request.

Media specialist Maxus took control of planning and programming for the marque's TV and cinema activity, brokering a deal where the *#soundwithpower* campaign would appear in cinemas alongside three of the biggest major blockbusters of the year. Maxus also devised and implemented innovative digital platforms to showcase and support the 're-mixing deck', including an exclusive three-month partnership with music site Spotify.

Showroom materials and heavyweight online support, consisting of online advertising as well as interactive ads for mobile, iPad and Spotify were created by digital agency Weapon7 (Figure 4). An engaging social media strand with bespoke content was driven by creative agency Holler, playing off event advertising and leveraging real social discussion. Holler also brought the context of 'sound with power' to life through exclusive interviews with Lewis Hamilton.

Figure 4. Using different platforms

ENJOYING A MAJOR WIN
The results not only met but surpassed the original targets.

1. Audience engagement

Visits to the website in just three months	354,219
Visitors completing the experience	75%
Average dwell time on site	Two minutes, 16 seconds.

2. Record engagement with the brand

Mercedes' online engagement (including all likes, shares, comments, re-tweets, posts etc. on any platform	453,845
Increase in online engagement	+71%
Increase in engagement on Twitter	+564%

3. Significant growth in interest in the E-Class

Increase in visits to E-Class section of Mercedes website	92%
E-Class brochures download increase	117%
E-Class test drive requests increase	80%

4. Reaching the target audience

Perceived age of driver post-exposure (pre= 43)	37
Competitive drivers who saw a positive impact on driver image	74%
Customers new to Mercedes-Benz	52%

Even more importantly, sales rose during the campaign period by 38%, compared to an increase in the sector overall of only 9%. This meant that, for the first time, the E-Class was selling more than both its key rivals. In addition, the return on investment was a notable 1.4:1.

All images appearing in this case study are reproduced by permission of Mercedes-Benz.

MACMILLAN
Striking the perfect note

SNAPSHOT
The campaign mounted by Macmillan Cancer Support resonated strongly with all its target audiences thanks to a single and moving insight.

AGENCY
VCCP

KEY INSIGHTS
- One of the UK's leading and most admired cancer charities wanted to highlight how it could help people living with cancer while seeking to attract wider support by clarifying just what its brand stood for.
- A well-coordinated and multi-channel campaign was built around the simple but effective message that when you have cancer 'you are not alone'.
- It achieved unprecedented levels of awareness for the charity, deepening the relationships with all its prospective audiences and boosting donations.

SUMMARY
In 2013 Macmillan decided it needed to make clear just what it did in relation to the other high-profile cancer charities. The resulting campaign was based on a powerful insight. Despite the fact that cancer will directly or indirectly affect most of us, too often it can feel like you're facing it alone, whether you are living with a diagnosis or caring for someone who is. The hope was that by saying something that resonated widely, it would motivate the people who needed the charity's help to get in touch and it would inspire those who could help to get involved.

The campaign kicked off with a new research report which attracted widespread coverage, with TV, print and digital advertising featuring the 'Not Alone' theme.

The website was used to encourage people to donate and also featured case studies, research and information about how to get involved while social media enabled people to share experiences. The result was not only record levels of awareness but a significant rise in donations.

CANCER IN THE UK

Every day 910 people in the UK are faced with the news that they have cancer. There are now more than two million people living with the diagnosis, and that is set to double over the next 20 years from a combination of an ageing population, improved diagnosis and treatment and changing lifestyles.

This presents an enormous challenge in terms of designing how cancer care will be delivered since increasingly it won't happen only in hospitals, clinics and surgeries but also in the home, on high streets and online. Individuals, families and communities: we'll all need to get more active in helping each other live with cancer.

Macmillan Cancer Support occupies the 'living with cancer' space. Charities such as Cancer Research UK and other specialists research cures and treatment while Marie Curie and local hospices focus on palliative care (looking after people whose cancer cannot be cured). Macmillan deals with everything in between.

The charity is most famous for its nurses, but it also encompasses other medical professionals such as doctors, radiographers, dieticians and occupational therapists, among others. Services such as a helpline, a wealth of information, grants and benefits advice, online communities, public policy and research on the impact of cancer also number among its activities.

In addition, Macmillan acts as a 'critical friend' of the National Health Service (NHS), working with multiple providers to redesign and improve cancer care across the UK. Almost all of this work – 99% – is funded through voluntary contributions.

It's an extraordinarily diverse and nuanced response to the highly varied challenges facing people living with cancer. And as those lives change, the nature of what Macmillan does needs to change too. It's testament to the extraordinary commitment of its people that it has become one of the UK's most loved and dependable charities. But those two characteristics – variety and dependability – present a challenge.

On the surface, its objectives are straightforward:
- Increase the number of people who receive support by calling the support line, going online or accessing the information services.
- Grow the number who give support and boost the value of their donations through individual spontaneous giving, direct debits, legacies and participating in fundraising events.
- Expand the definition of 'giving' to encompass volunteering, campaigning for change, sharing experiences with someone who needs it and being there for someone in their life.

These objectives are encapsulated by the theme underpinning the brand: 'Inspire millions to get involved'. But it has been complicated by four factors:
- Macmillan is by its very nature diverse. The brand has never had the equivalent vision of something like Cancer Research UK's 'Together we will beat cancer' to capture why it exists and why people should donate.
- Also, unlike Cancer Research UK, the majority of Macmillan's past advertising expenditure had been steered toward messages of 'getting' support rather than 'giving' support. It was seen as something of a stalwart friend, particularly through its nurses, and hence a brand that someone needed rather than one that needed anything for itself. This lack of urgency was an issue for fundraising.
- To increase this sense of urgency, the obvious response was to raise the level of emotional intensity. But Macmillan was determined never to let a drive for funds cause any sense of demeaning of those it helped or prevent them from seeking that help. If a harrowing ad was made about cancer, it might attract donations, but at what cost to those currently living with a diagnosis? At the same time, emphasising how vulnerable its services were might make people hesitate before getting in touch.
- For any spending to be effective, there needed to be a single campaign that worked for all audiences and gave clearly-distinctive calls to action. In other words, it had to encourage people both to give and to get support.

FINDING THE INSIGHT
Any campaign had to be grounded in an insight that brought together four vital elements:
1. People living with cancer, or caring for someone who has it, would have to see something of themselves.
2. Those unaffected by cancer would have to be moved by the emotion conveyed.
3. Macmillan would have to show how it could help.

4. To really inspire millions, everyone would have to see how they could help in their own way.

It wouldn't be easy. How could a single thought not only express but also dignify and empathise with such a wide range of human emotions and experience? After all, the fact that over 900 people are diagnosed every day, plus the thousands who love them, means that every story is intensely personal and refracted through personal experiences.

The first step was to read and re-read the research, from clinical data on survival rates to brand insights and reports on charitable giving. Focus groups were carried out with people living with cancer, while immersion in the 'world' of Macmillan included talking to nurses, listening to calls, visiting information centres and spending time with the online community.

One striking finding stood out: despite the fact that cancer will directly or indirectly affect most of us, too often it can feel like you're facing it alone, whether you are living with a diagnosis or caring for someone who is.

This can arise from any number of reasons, from the physical effects of the treatment, finding it hard to talk to family and friends about it or missing work or school to having less money to do the things you normally would. It can come from feeling treated as a condition rather than a person, or just not knowing where to turn.

This was where Macmillan could come into its own. The charity couldn't take away the pain, the fear or sadness but what it could do is help people feel less alone which research showed was universal.

That led to the thought that was simple but compelling and irrefutable: no one should face cancer alone (Figure 1).

Figure 1. The compelling insight

GETTING THE MESSAGE HEARD

The 'Not Alone' campaign went public in February 2013 and translated seamlessly into a wide array of activities made possible by the tireless work of Macmillan's extensive community of volunteers and partners.

Figure 2. Clip from TV campaign

Figure 3. Clip from TV campaign

Key features included:
- Opening the campaign by publicising a new research report, *Facing the Fight Alone*, that brought widespread news coverage.
- An above-the-line campaign that broke nationally on TV, in print and digitally (Figures 2–6).

Figure 4. The campaign

Figure 5. The campaign

Figure 6. The campaign

- The website stimulated donations and gave the campaign more weight through case studies, research and information on how to get involved.
- Social media helped share comments about the campaign and encouraged people to talk about their own experiences.
- New information leaflets were published about the issues raised in the campaign, as well as promoting services, volunteering opportunities and advice.

- Merchandising attracted donations and a sense of belonging.
- The message was integrated into key fundraising pushes, the promotion of services, healthcare professional activities, local volunteering, fundraising and briefing papers.

ACHIEVING NEW LEVELS OF ENGAGEMENT
Tracking levels showed that levels of recognition were well above target, with peak awareness measures 66% higher than any previous campaign (Figure 7). A range of moving comments on YouTube accompanying the video showed just how strongly the message had resonated among those affected in some way by the disease

TV advertising, peak levels of recognition (Affected)

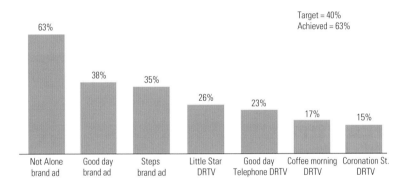

Figure 7. Levels of recognition

The awareness also translated into action:
- By the end of the year the TV campaign had already directly resulted in 22,000 text donations and over 12,000 additional donations.
- Econometric modelling demonstrated that the 'get support' TV message was 10% more effective than the previous campaign in driving calls to the support helpline.
- There was a record number of visits to the website. Modelling showed that more than 500,000 of these could be attributed to the TV ad alone.
- Facebook engagement spiked 40-fold with the campaign launch, with the 'number of people talking about this' jumping from 1,000 to over 40,000. Baseline Facebook activity more than doubled.

Macmillan Cancer Support named best charity brand of 2013

22 August 2013 by Jenna Pudelek, Be the First to Comment

The cancer support charity knocks Cancer Research UK off the top of the annual Third Sector Charity Brand Index

Figure 8. Best charity of the year

Figure 9. World's biggest coffee morning

There were also benefits for the brand itself:

- In 2013 it was named best charity of the year in the annual Third Sector Charity Brand Index, knocking Cancer Research UK off the top spot (Figure 8).
- The likelihood to donate among those currently unaffected by cancer jumped over 10 percentage points from the campaign launch.

Significantly, the campaign has had a longer-lasting impact on the charity's fortunes. For instance, one of its key events, the World's Biggest Coffee Morning, saw a dramatic increase in revenue in 2013 from £15 to £20 million (Figure 9). Finally, the theme of 'Not Alone' has led to further research into isolation which will in turn bring greater insight and influence the future provision of Macmillan's services.

All images appearing in this case study are reproduced by permission of Macmillan Cancer Support.

CHAPTER 2

02

Connecting with customers

The beauty of marketing in the 21st century is the abundance of tools we have to connect with customers. However, we also need the creativity to make the most of these tools, alongside the rigour and honesty about the insights we uncover and the tenacity and leadership to develop customer propositions and execute brilliantly. Not an easy task!

Each of the brands in these case studies were at different stages of maturity in the development of the relationships with their customers. They are striking examples of how to use the right tools at the right time to strengthen those relationships.

Notcutts really did understand what was important for their customers and developed a rich programme – not just a loyalty card – to reward and deepen further the customers' relationship with its brand. That led to a virtuous circle of value for the whole organisation from the data collected.

O_2 devised the language and reward mechanism that motivated their customers and genuinely connected them to the brand.

easyJet was determined to move beyond a transactional relationship based on a price-response model to build long-term brand value. This is more than a marketing campaign but the genuine beginning of a new way to connect with customers.

Finally, Aviva needed a different sort of conversation with its advisers in response to an external market change. It invested in really understanding its audience and creatively employing a number of tools to reshape the changing relationship.

Elizabeth Fagan
Marketing Director,
Health & Beauty,
International and Brands
Alliance Boots

TELEFONICA O_2
Setting a new benchmark for brand loyalty

SNAPSHOT

Telefonica O_2's Priority Moments became one of the UK's fastest-growing loyalty programmes and cut customer churn considerably.

AGENCY

Cherry London

KEY INSIGHTS

- Telefonica O_2 needed to create a loyalty programme to strengthen bonds with customers in one of industry's most fickle markets.
- Priority Moments took hold with such a grip that five Priority Moments were redeemed with participating brands every minute of every day.
- Not only was churn significantly reduced, but customer advocacy of the brand had a beneficial impact on the bottom line.

SUMMARY

Telefonica O_2 is one of the UK's leading mobile operators. Facing an unforgiving market with little customer loyalty, in 2011 it decided to embark on an ambitious loyalty programme to strengthen customer bonds with the brand.

The result was Priority Moments, a mobile loyalty programme that uses real-time insight and targeting to provide O_2 customers with special offers from their preferred brands such as Marks & Spencer (M&S), New Look and Debenhams via their mobile phones (through apps, mobile websites, online and MMS/SMS). These are based on their interests, behaviour and location.

It became very successful very quickly. By 2012 registrations had doubled, making it the UK's fastest-growing loyalty programme. It was also made available to small and medium-sized businesses so that they could make offers more local and hence relevant for customers. Just 18 months from launch, Priority Moments had delivered a significant reduction in churn, with five Priority Moments being redeemed by O_2 customers every minute of every day.

LOOKING FOR LOYALTY

Telefonica O_2 UK operates in arguably the most fiercely competitive mobile market in the world, with numerous operators and mobile virtual network operators (MVNOs) all trying to achieve market leadership. The market is a difficult one: it suffers from high churn, increasing subscriber acquisition costs (SAC), limited differentiation and low customer engagement and loyalty. This is driven by consumer demand for heavily subsidised and increasingly costly handsets in the intense battle for new customers.

Telefonica O_2 UK was determined to meet these challenges by making customers their priority through an innovative new location-based mobile loyalty programme, Priority Moments, which complemented its acclaimed Priority Ticketing service. Priority Moments, launched in July 2011, provides O_2 customers with targeted offers and exclusive, targeted rewards from brands they love via their mobile phones (app, mobile web, online and MMS/ SMS), based on their interests, behaviour, and most importantly where they are. Rewards can be redeemed in-store and online (Figure 1).

The brief for partnership marketing agency Cherry London had been demanding: create a loyalty programme that customers would engage with every day, offering

Figure 1. Priority Moments

outstanding value in a tough economic climate, yet dramatically different from the multitude of 'daily deal' sites that had saturated the market. O_2 wanted to give its customers something they couldn't get anywhere else.

There were a number of challenging objectives:
- Make Priority Moments the best and most-used mobile loyalty programme in the UK.
- Reach and reward more O_2 customers.
- Drive more frequent engagement.
- Drive customer advocacy of O_2 measured by customer service index (CSI) and reduce churn.
- Strengthen brand perceptions: increase scores for consideration, attractiveness and value for money.

A JOURNEY OF DISCOVERY
The Priority Moments journey began by talking to O_2 customers to understand what really mattered to them. This insight informed the structure and content of the Priority Moments programme and continues to do so with ongoing bespoke research, social media tracking and behavioural analysis.

In order to target and influence customers positively, both qualitative focus research and quantitative research into customer preferences and behaviour were used to identify all the things that mattered to them, such as:
- Their favourite brands.
- Moments when they needed a boost e.g. Monday mornings, or the last few weeks of the school holidays.
- Celebratory moments e.g. birthdays (personal or anniversary of being with O_2).

The research also helped reveal the moments in their relationship with O_2 when their attitude shifted, evidenced by a dip in the net promoter score (NPS), for example, and the risk of churn increased, while customers were also segmented based on value (tenure and spend).

This understanding led to the creation of a tiered reward structure and a targeted approach based on value, using real-time location-based insights, which included:
- Extraordinary moments
- Extraordinary offers
- Headline moments
- To say thank you

Each type of reward performed a special function, including to encourage everyday engagement, acquire or re-activate a lapsed user, reward customers based on their spend and tenure and to increase overall satisfaction with O_2 (Figure 2).

Figure 2. A comprehensive approach

MAKING IT WORK
These rewards demanded careful execution.

1. Extraordinary moments
These were unmissable experiences, content and rewards that couldn't be found anywhere else, which created extraordinary moments for thousands of customers, rather than just a lucky few. For example:
• To celebrate the Jubilee: a free pair of Union Jack flip flops from BHS.
• An upgrade on the Heathrow Express and an airport lounge pass.
• A free lunch with Priority Moments at a popular food chain.
• The chance to get a new game or DVD release before anyone else at HMV.

Figure 3. 'Priority Moments' extraordinary offers

2. Extraordinary offers

These consisted of exclusive offers giving O$_2$ customers real value and savings on everyday items and more occasional treats (Figure 3):

- £1 for a pizza and unlimited salad at Pizza Hut.
- Four free Millie's Cookies.
- M&S 'Dine in' for £8.
- 50% off movie tickets at Odeon.
- 20% off at Toni & Guy hair salons – the first time in 40 years the company had run a national discount.
- Buy one pair of shoes at Office for the party season, get another pair for free.

By the end of 2012 Priority Moments had saved O$_2$ customers on average £35-£40 per month and substantially increased customers' perceptions of the 'value for money' they received.

3. To say thank-you

Targeted rewards based on value segment were sent to thank O$_2$ customers for their loyalty on their two-year anniversary with O$_2$ when NPS typically dipped, or just to surprise them. Customers were targeted via SMS/MMS and collected their personal 'thank-you' via the Priority Moments app, or mobile web site:

- A Caffè Nero iced coffee on a hot day just to say thank-you.
- A £5-£20 mobile gift card to spend at Debenhams.
- A handpicked gift box from Hotel Chocolat.

4. Headline moments

This was a package of unmissable rewards to create excitement and a sense of urgency at a key moment such as Christmas, where O$_2$ could help customers make the most of the festive season (Figure 4). For instance, for Christmas 2012 an Advent Calendar was created made up of 24 extraordinary rewards, exclusive content and outstanding offers:

- Christmas master-class with renowned chef Jean-Christophe Novelli, giving customers tips on how to create the perfect Christmas dinner and £25 off all the ingredients with Ocado (over 400,000 YouTube views).

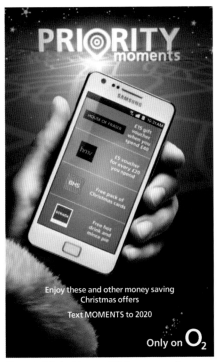

Figure 4. 'Priority Moments' Christmas campaign

- A free de-icer and scraper from Halfords executed in a timely manner: when it snowed.
- 30% off at New Look.
- £10 to spend on Christmas presents at The Fragrance Shop.
- Exclusive shopping events at Bluewater shopping centre.

A PERFECT FIT

To fuel Priority Moments, partnerships were developed with some of the UK's leading brands (Odeon, M&S, Debenhams, New Look, Caffè Nero and WH Smith, to name a few). These were the ones O$_2$ customers loved, the ones that did things differently, and the ones that didn't promote themselves to death (Figure 5).

Figure 5. 'Priority Moments' partnerships

To secure these high profile strategic partnerships for 12 months and secure significant investment in kind, many even before launch, a mutually-beneficial partner proposition was developed:

- Tiered investment and media packages with guaranteed outcomes.
- Measurable and defined benefits from their investment, with in-depth tracking, analysis of respondents, and, most importantly, sales tracking.
- A flexible and controllable management platform, built by R/GA London, which allowed for a range of experiences and offers to be promoted with different redemption mechanics and controls (i.e. unique codes, 'redeem once' functionality, limits per customer etc.) and daily reporting.
- A closed-loop evaluation system to track the success of each offer for O$_2$ and partners, as well as popularity with customers.

Priority Moments was launched in July 2011 with 20 strategic partners, and soon grew to over 150 partners. In July 2012, O$_2$ extended Priority Moments to small-and medium-sized enterprises (SMEs) to make the proposition more local and more relevant to customers. This was supported by the development of a self-service platform, again developed by R/GA London, that enabled local businesses to upload and target O$_2$ customers with relevant offers. There were now over 1,000 SMEs promoting local offers on Priority Moments by the end of 2012.

CONCLUSIVE RESULTS
Priority Moments needed to prove its value quickly and show considerable growth in 2012. Its success far exceeded expectations across all measures.

A. Increase advocacy of O$_2$ and reduce churn
- The initiative generated significant incremental churn benefit.
- Heavily-active users had a much lower annualised churn.
- Registered customers with low active use saw a churn reduction.
- Positive CSI, with scores much higher than those not aware.
- Value for money metrics increased for O$_2$ customers.
- Customer consideration of O$_2$ increased for existing and prospective customers.
- The 'Millie's Cookie' offer attracted thousands of favourable tweets.

B. Reach and reward more customers
- Registrations doubled in 2012, making it the UK's fastest-growing loyalty programme.
- Over one billion offers had been viewed by year-end.
- 75 offers were viewed every second of the day.
- Every minute of every day O$_2$ customers redeemed five Priority Moments.
- It saved customers on average £35-£40 per month – a total of £35-£40 million

across registered customers (based on the top five performing Priority Moments offers each month and the average saving).
- It had the highest number of rewards and exclusive 'free gifts' versus the competition and not linked to spend.
- Customers could redeem up to £218 worth of free gifts across the year (O$_2$ internal survey across all offers available).
- Customers could have saved well over £1,000 from Priority Moments in 2012 alone – more than twice the average phone bill.
- Scores for key brand metrics over time, including consideration, attractiveness and value for money, all rose well above targets.

C. Registrants with Priority Moments
- In 2012, registrants of Priority Moments increased over 100%.

D. Frequent engagement with Priority Moments
- In 2012, Priority Moments' active base (those customers that used Priority Moments at least once in the last 30 days) doubled.

E. Return on marketing expenditure
- The significant marketing investment to develop the mobile platform and launch a loyalty programme of this scale paid off handsomely, with a notable reduction in churn and incremental revenue that delivered clear return on the investment.

All images appearing in this case study are reproduced by permission of Telefonica O$_2$.

NOTCUTTS
Cultivating a gardener's delight

SNAPSHOT

The family-owned group of garden centres designed an inspirational loyalty scheme which had a far-reaching impact on brand and financial performance.

AGENCIES

babyGRAND Marketing and Coniak

KEY INSIGHTS

- Notcutts wanted to reward its most loyal customers and attract new ones in a competitive and relatively undifferentiated market.
- Its Sage Privilege Club became a model for how to develop a fee-based loyalty scheme by careful use of customer segmentation and targeted communications.
- Membership fees alone brought in an extra £2.5 million into the business over three years, with club members accounting for 40% of profits overall by the end of the first year.

SUMMARY

Family-owned Notcutts Garden Centre Group, with a history stretching back to the late 19th century, operates garden centres across England and prides itself on its value, service, range and expertise. Faced with competition not only from independent garden centres but also from groups operated by some of the biggest retailers, the company was determined to find a way to engage more closely with its loyal customers and grow the customer base overall.

The solution was to set up a reward scheme that was far more than just a discount card. The Sage Privilege Club would give members a 10% discount on every purchase they made during the year, with an additional £85 worth of benefits. However, for this to be cost-effective, an annual fee would have to be charged.

The pilot scheme run to test out this concept proved to be a winner, with 7,000 people signing up. For the full roll-out, Notcutts' target of 75,000 members in the first year was reached in six months. By the end of 2012, the company had signed up one in five of its customers for the club, which generated £2.5 million in membership fees alone. Significantly, Sage members were accounting for 40% of Notcutts' profits by the end of the first year.

STANDING OUT IN A CLUTTERED LANDSCAPE

The garden centre retail sector is formed predominantly of one-off independently-owned garden centres. There are also around half a dozen garden centre groups of note, with the top three being Wyevale, now venture capital-owned and called The Garden Centre Group, Tesco subsidiary Dobbies and family-owned Notcutts (Figure 1). Garden centre customers are typically keen gardeners. They are educated, knowledgeable and more likely to be female than male. Many customers, particularly

Figure 1.

the older ones, also have time on their hands and a repertoire of garden centres that they frequently visit. That said, Notcutts knew it had a core of very loyal customers that it wanted to reward, protect and engage with, within the framework of a bigger base of loyal customers for the long term.

This led to a new strategy for the business: to ring-fence and develop its most valuable gardeners and to capture a greater share of their wallet. To do this, the retailer needed the answers to some searching questions:
- How do we show that we offer our customers exceptional value, service, range and expertise, so we make it worth their while shopping only with Notcutts?
- In particular, what could we do to increase the average number of visits to a garden centre from five to six per year, which is the UK national average? (Source: Horticultural Trades Association.)
- How do we share our knowledge and expertise as a garden centre brand?
- And, finally, how do we tap into our customers' love of gardening and build our ability to have one-to-one relationships with them?

Notcutts knew the answer lay in gaining as much knowledge about its customers as possible and that email and direct marketing represented the best and most cost-effective way of talking to customers – if only it could get enough data. Reward schemes in 2009 were not unusual. The company's key competitors already had clubs and point schemes and it was well aware of how powerful they could be for a business. It decided that it wanted to build one that was market-leading.

The team was a collaboration of the in-house marketing team, agency specialists and data analysts. The goal was to turn fickle but valuable gardeners into brand converts who would shop at Notcutts regularly and as a first choice, thus increasing frequency of visit and increasing average transaction value (ATV). The aim was to bring in incremental revenues of approximately £1 million in year one, make marketing communications cost effective with a positive return on investment (ROI) and gain actionable insights through testing. And, on top of all that, to build a scheme that could improve management information and aid planning across the entire business.

The scheme also had to be capable of selling itself as the company had limited launch funds, relying on marketing through point-of-sale (POS) in the garden centre, and additional staff support. Therefore it was agreed that to achieve real prominence, a brand would be created in its own right while still clearly belonging to and sharing Notcutts' values.

WELCOME TO THE CLUB

It was decided that the scheme should be very much a 'privilege club' as opposed to just a discount, money-off card – a scheme customers felt had greater value than just the savings they would make as a member. It also needed to be a scheme that had real depth. The result was a club called the Sage Privilege Club, which offered every member 10% off every purchase every day for their full year's membership (Figure 2).

Figure 2. Sage Privilege Club

The value this offered was significant. On top of this there were more than £85 worth of other benefits to be given to members throughout the year. Financial modelling told Notcutts that to offer these market-leading benefits an annual fee would have to be charged. But – and this was the hard bit – could the company get its customers to pay to be a member when some of the biggest schemes in the sector were free to join – like Wyevale's, for example?

A pilot was run at the end of 2009 in three of the garden centres. After four weeks it was clear the club was working, with all six-week target key performance indicators (KPIs) already being exceeded by a large margin. There were 7,000 sign-ups, which, over the four-week period, brought in an incremental £100,000.

For roll-out the company planned on having 75,000 members by the end of the first year (approximately one in 10 customers). This was achieved in six months. By the end of the first year, Sage customers had contributed 40% of the profit for the whole Notcutts business (Figure 3).

Figure 3. Profits

REALISING THE REWARDS

The long-term results were compelling in a number of critical areas.

1. Customer lifetime value
Sage's success was dependent on increasing frequency and value. The data showed that the three-year value of a Sage member was £670 compared to £200 from non-Sage members.

2. Segmentation

The company wanted to understand who its loyal (frequent and valuable) members were, and so created a recency/frequency value (RFV) model. Among other things, it revealed that over 30% of all sales from Sage members were coming from just 11% of members. This 'very high' segment was categorised by a spend over £150 in a 12-month period, with more than six visits to the garden centre in the same time frame.

When it came to renewal, Notcutts knew that those who had spent more were more likely to renew. So it brought in a communications programme that would target selected members mid-year to encourage their spend levels (Figures 4 and 5).

Figure 4. Targeted communications

Figure 5. Targeted communications

- It targeted those who at week 38 of their annual membership and were at a level of spend that implied (from historical data) that their renewal rates would be at best 35%.
- It also targeted those who had spent more than this threshold at week 38, but who had not made a garden centre visit for over six weeks.

The promotional element to this trigger programme was a spend-and-save voucher, using the knowledge of the average transaction value of the targeted members. The initial sign of success came with the voucher redemption rate across a six-week validity period of 45%. The number of transactions was 20% higher in the contacted groups, compared to a representative control, with average transaction value coming in £5.50 higher even after allowing for the voucher. Even more importantly, 5% more customers renewed at the end of their membership year than in the control.

3. Improved value for customers

By the end of 2012, the average member's annual saving was now running at £14.28 net of the annual membership fee of £10. This was calculated by taking the fixed 10% discount, the redemption of restaurant offers and use of other Privilege Club benefits across the 12-month period. In addition, members received several free gifts across the year. Sage members really appreciated the Club's benefits and consequently they helped shift buying behaviour (Figures 6, 7, 8):

Figures 6 and 7.

Figure 8.

- The free tea and coffee offered to members each month resulted in 700,000 redemptions across the customer base per annum. This represented over 60% redemption for all active members.
- Over a year, 50,000 members attended the '20% off everything' shopping events run bi-annually.
- These now represented two of the company's highest income weekends of the year.

- The average number of buy-one-get-one-free (BOGOF) redemptions in the restaurants (given to members three times per year) totalled 60,000 per annum.

These deals were planned to drive traffic at quiet times of the year and structured so that Notcutts was still profit-positive, despite the promotion offered. In addition, all high-value price-pointing in the garden centres carried the Sage Privilege Club price, so members could easily see how much they were saving (which also encouraged more members into the scheme).

4. Increasing revenues
The club proved very profitable for the business:
- Membership fees alone brought in an extra £2.5 million into the business in three years, which after costs represented £2 million for the company.
- In addition, having customers as Sage members was better for Notcutts than having them as just regular customers. They were more active and on average were bigger spenders so the retention programme was critical. Members were targeted six weeks before their renewal date with a series of tried and tested communications. There was also a reactivation process that targeted any lapsed high spenders.
- What was a fee-based club without direct debit constantly exceeded targets, with renewals running at an impressive 60%. By the second year renewal rates were actually exceeding 70%.

FAR-REACHING EFFECTS
As of the end of December 2012 the Sage Privilege Club had 122,327 paying current active members. This represented one in five of all Notcutts' customers nationally.
- Moreover, the whole business benefited from the Sage Privilege Club. It not only helped the buying and merchandising team with their planning during category reviews, but Notcutts was now able to introduce certain lines into some of its garden centres based on a clearer understanding of the customer profile.
- It helped ring-fence and develop the most valuable gardening customers over the past three years. Against the market average of five garden centre visits per year, the visiting frequency of Sage members had increased by a multiple of over 1.5 per year on average.
- Finally, customers engaged with the company more, as Notcutts was front of mind when they were making a decision on which garden centre to visit. They were also given new products to test, with their reviews shared with the rest of the membership.

All images appearing in this case study are reproduced by permission of Notcutts.

EASYJET
Working a marketing miracle

SNAPSHOT

A sweeping shift in the marketing strategy from a traditional price/response model to a more long-term brand-focused one had a far-reaching impact on the airline's brand and business.

AGENCIES
VCCP, OMD UK, Havas EHS

KEY INSIGHTS

- easyJet's traditional price/response marketing strategy was no longer as effective as it had been in an environment of recession, changing competitive threats and higher operating costs.
- The airline bravely decided to focus on a brand-building customer-centric model that would distinguish it from its low-cost rivals.
- The resulting marketing strategy not only substantially altered customer perceptions and increased brand consideration but it led to an unprecedented share price rise.
- Even more notably, all this was achieved with no net additional marketing budget.

SUMMARY

easyJet is the UK's largest airline. Founded in 1995 with a call centre operation and just two routes, it now boasts over 200 aircraft travelling over 600 routes across 30 countries and transporting more than 60 million passengers a year.

However, in 2010 the airline faced a number of challenges. The effects of the recession, coupled with higher fuel prices, were increasing the airline's operating costs just as customers were demanding the lowest possible fares for their holiday flights – or, worse, not taking holidays at all. The company needed to develop a positioning for the brand that looked beyond a model based almost solely on pricing.

The result was a bold repositioning from a pure low-cost proposition, to a customer-centric, affinity-driving brand. The media strategy also shifted radically, from what had been a more traditional price/response model to a longer-term brand building strategy centred on the campaign theme 'Europe by easyJet'.

Resulting improvements in brand perception, consideration and conversion reaped extraordinary commercial dividends. The role of marketing in this transformation was critical: the combined impact of the new direction and significant efficiency improvements meant that marketing's annual financial contribution to the company increased by 134% to £203 million, a return on investment (ROI) of 6:1.

A BUSINESS MODEL UNDER THREAT
In 2010 easyJet was facing the deepest Europe-wide recession in living history, at a time of sky rocketing fuel prices (Figure 1). Operational costs were therefore increasing, just as customers were demanding the lowest possible fares for their holiday flights, or even not taking holidays at all.

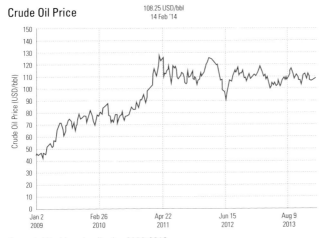

Figure 1. World crude oil price 2009-2013

In addition, the company was caught in a fierce competitive battle from both sides. The traditional flag carriers were cutting their prices and stripping back services as they attempted to adopt the same low-cost model easyJet had pioneered. And, at the bottom of the market, price promotion was rife.

When the airline launched in 1995, it had promised to make flying "as cheap as buying a pair of jeans". As a result, marketing had necessarily spent fifteen years communicating price at the expense of almost anything else. The brand personality ranged from the controversial to the predictably formulaic, reinforcing consumers' "cheap" perceptions. But a brand positioning based solely on cost-leadership and discount flying was no longer viable when easyJet was increasingly no longer the cheapest.

However, the company also realised that this could be an opportunity, not a threat. Currently the marketing strategy represented a significant disconnect from the reality of the brand experience. Correcting this represented a sizeable chance to build a significantly more positive brand image with long-term equity and the potential to attract a much wider audience.

WASTING LITTLE TIME

Airlines are extraordinarily complex organisations and easyJet was no exception. Spanning more than 40 countries and 8,500 employees, major initiatives to transform punctuality and roll out 'allocated seating' would take time to come to fruition. Marketing, however, could be refreshed relatively quickly. This became an advantage of exceptional importance.

From an external perspective, the migration to a customer-focused brand-building strategy needed to prove rapidly that it could not only still do the job of driving short-term sales targets, but also generate higher revenue and profit. From an internal culture perspective, it needed to be an important symbol for a radical shift in mindset and set the tone for the brand's new personality and behaviour.

It was without doubt a complex proposition: the marketing needed to demonstrate a transition to a brand that was closer by association to premium flag carriers, while at the same time maintaining the democratic challenger spirit appeal and pride in the brand's low-cost heritage.

To deliver this, the marketing team created an internal proposition: "To deliver ease and affordability to our customers", which would guide every new customer experience improvement over the next three years.

BEING RESOURCEFUL ABOUT RESOURCES

The shift in focus from tactical direct response advertising to a more emotional brand-building approach necessitated a radical change in the media mix. The company had traditionally been a heavy print, outdoor and digital advertiser, with cost efficiency as the primary objective. However TV, with its strength as an emotional brand-building channel, became an obvious ambition, particularly with the aim of widening reach and increasing penetration outside the usual customer base.

The tricky part was that adding TV would be expensive. With no extra marketing investment on the table, the options were to sacrifice another channel, which could risk day-to-day sales performance, or to find the budget through ingenuity.

The solution was to apply rigorous hypothesis testing, particularly to the digital advertising spend, which represented 76% of the media investment. The key actions undertaken included:
- Testing the hypothesis that bidding on brand terms in Google Search delivered zero incremental sales. This hypothesis turned out to be correct, with the result of saving £3.97 million per annum.
- Reducing digital network partners from fourteen to three, thus eliminating unnecessary duplication and resulting in an annual spend reduction of £2.09 million and a cost-per-sale improvement of 81%.
- Developing a "search playbook" to match commercial data with pay-per-click (PPC) keyword data, ensuring that PPC investments were only made for keywords that supported routes under plan.
- Trialling a new personalised approach to customer relationship marketing (CRM) newsletters, which resulted in 30% more revenue from marketable contacts (see box, 'Making the customer experience more personal').

(All data from BrandScience/easyJet Econometrics 2010-13)

The resulting efficiency savings of more than £6 million per year created a war chest to assign to brand-building activity. Television would become the lead communications channel, but there were now also sufficient funds to use high-impact outdoor, sponsorship, promotions, experiential and social channels.

MAKING THE CUSTOMER EXPERIENCE MORE PERSONAL
By focusing the business on the customer experience, easyJet wanted to differentiate itself from other budget airlines and create incremental revenue not just through hard sales, but through a memorable and positive traveller programme.

The result was built on the easyJet brand proposition 'where are you going?' to ignite the natural feelings of anticipation travellers have during the countdown to their next trip. easyJet would provide help and inspiration at each milestone during the pre-flight experience and ultimately transform a functional, hard-sell approach into an engaging conversation.

Because of the dynamic capability of the programme, the company was able to tailor the content both visually and tonally to a high degree. A clear distinction was made between vital information people 'needed to know', information that was 'nice to know' and 'inspiring content' to enhance travellers' experiences.

The overall objectives were to:
• Increase opportunities to talk with customers to provide useful and practical information before the flight, but also with suggestions for an improved journey.
• Decrease marketing investment while increasing its efficiency at every touchpoint.

The measured objectives were to:
• Increase engagement with the emails.
• Increase online check-in.
• Increase ancillaries and extra service revenue.

Within the first ten months the pre-flight programme had been delivered to 36 million travellers, leading to a return on investment of 199:1. The 'open' rates were more than double travel sector benchmarks. As easyJet CEO Carolyn McCall noted, "Email is now driving close to 70% more revenue against the same period last year. Emailed customers are 20% more valuable and book 11% more frequently than non-email customers."

DARING TO BE DIFFERENT

The next challenge was deciding the message. While low-cost competitors such as Ryanair continued to create advertising centred around low prices, easyJet recognised that its premium flag carrier competitors continued to fixate on the in-flight service experience (partly to continue justifying the price premium). This, by its very nature, emphasised functional messages despite the gloss. As a no-frills airline, the airline would never be able to compete on this level, which freed it up to talk about something much more interesting.

After all, the real benefit of easyJet was to help more people travel to more places, more often. It was not just about selling seats. It was about selling Europe and all the exciting experiences it had to offer. This became the focus of the advertising: championing the experience at the destination.

It led to the development of the new long-term brand platform 'Europe by easyJet' which allowed the brand to create emotional affinity with the target audience and be more aspirational in its look and feel (Figure 2).

Figure 2. Europe by easyJet campaign 2011

At the same time, the marketing team was keen to avoid appearing self-indulgent and weaken the sales-driving role of its marketing activity. A mandatory feature of every execution was that the low-cost credentials would continue to be reinforced by promoting a low price.

The aim was indeed ambitious: it wasn't limited simply to showing a warmer, more customer-centric side of the company through the advertising. easyJet was committed to proving, as quickly as possible, that its commitment to transforming the customer experience was both genuine and achievable. While punctuality improvements and the trial of allocated seating would take longer to be fully operational, the marketing team was able to develop a number of tools characterised by a level of innovation and quality which far outstripped expectations of what a low-cost airline might deliver.

From the award-winning mobile app, to choosing and booking tools such as 'Inspire Me', a series of seamless and enjoyable interactions were created which did much to widen easyJet's appeal. In addition, within the first 12 months of the campaign, easyJet invested heavily in a website re-design, which transformed the user experience, but also delivered a category-leading level of transparency in terms of pricing and additional charges.

Within six months of rolling out these new marketing-led customer experience improvements, easyJet was able to provide evidence to investors that this new strategy was already delivering an instant return on investment. As CEO Carolyn McCall stated in the 2011 annual report, "easyJet launched its new advertising campaign 'Europe by easyJet' (and) we have seen promising initial results from the campaign with a 250% increase in customers describing themselves as 'much more likely to buy from easyJet'".

In the same report the company was also able to point to a 8.5% year-on-year (YOY) increase in unique visitors to the website of 213 million. By 2012 easyJet.com had become the company's biggest sales channel and had become the world's third most-searched-for airline.

INTRODUCING GENERATION EASYJET

The initial and crucial important step in easyJet's evolution to emotional equity-building advertising was now well established. The first two years' results were clearly indicating that this shift had been successful, both from a brand and business perspective. However, the company wasn't finished yet.

The next phase in its brand journey was moving from a territory of championing the experience at the destination, which was emotionally powerful but category generic, into something which easyJet could 'own'. It took inspiration from the easyJet staff and customers, who had become increasingly diverse as the brand attracted more business travellers, empty-nesters and affluent second-home owners. It identified among them a common spirit despite their differences in age, nationality and background – a 'get up and go' mindset that had seen them embrace the opportunity of low-cost air travel to do more, see more, and go more often.

The company called them 'generation easyJet' and created a new, evolved campaign that shifted its focus away from just the destination and to the mindset and attitudes of this newly-emerging generation (Figure 3). And, now that the offer could promote allocated seating fully and outstanding punctuality figures, a dedicated campaign targeting business travellers was created: "Business Sense".

It alluded to the tension between the old establishment and the modern generation of agile businessmen and women: those who valued punctuality and value far more than getting a gin and tonic onboard.

Figure 3. 2013 generation easyJet campaign

TRANSFORMING THE BRAND AND THE BUSINESS

The easyJet brand journey was remarkably successful in delivering tangible results for both the brand and business.

Perceptions of the brand improved exponentially, according to GfK brand tracking 2011-2013:

- easyJet nearly doubled its consideration score.
- Twice as many people considered easyJet "a brand for me", said that they cared about the airline, expressed loyalty and believed that easyJet "understands why I travel" (Figure 4).

Championing people's hearts

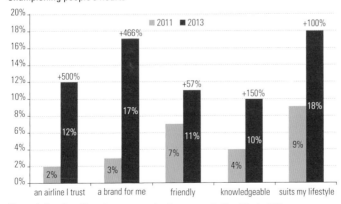

Figure 4. Emotional brand engagement   Source: easyJet Brand Tracker/GfK

This shift in perception directly pushed brand preference and propensity to book. Upon seeing the campaign, almost +27% more people said they were more likely to purchase from easyJet. Overall, across all markets, one in five now considered easyJet as their first choice airline – a significant jump from just one in 10 in 2011 (Figures 5 and 6).

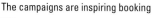
The campaigns are inspiring booking

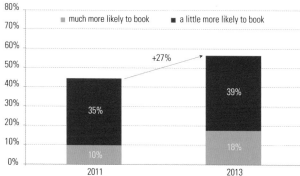

Figure 5. Campaign impact on buying intentions   Source: easyJet Brand Tracker/GfK

easyJet as first choice is on the up

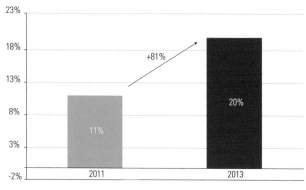

Figure 6. Brand preference rises   Source: easyJet Brand Tracker/GfK

Since 2010, easyJet's overall revenue grew an impressive +26% against a market growth (by passenger numbers) of just 10% (Figure 7). This was not just a function of increased capacity (about +15%) but also the willingness of the customers attracted to pay more, with revenue per seat growing over the period by +13.2% and incremental seat sales rising significantly (Figure 8).

Revenue (£billions)

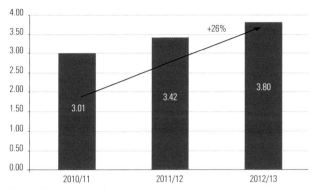

Figure 7. Revenue growth   Source: easyJet annual report 2013

Incremental seat sales (millions)

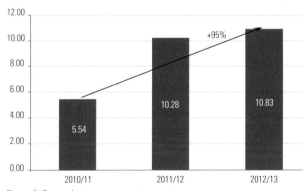

Figure 8. Seat sales   BrandScience Econometrics 2013

In particular, it was a reflection of easyJet's success in attracting an entirely new segment of customers: the business traveller. Accounting for just 5% of their customer base in 2010, business now represented over 20% and continues to grow.

The number of passengers flying with easyJet reached a record high of over 60 million in 2013. Econometrics has demonstrated that the new communications approach delivered +95.5% growth in incremental seat sales via paid media across the period, despite a decrease in overall media investment (2010 – 2013).

Marketing activity became significantly more efficient. Increases in consideration and revenue were achieved despite a 16% reduction in above-the-line media spend between 2010- 2013, resulting in a 23.5% reduction in marketing spend per seat booked.

The decision to invest in the development of a category-leading mobile app also paid off, with 7.7 million downloads now contributing 6.4% of easyJet's total e-commerce revenue. Development of a simpler, more customer friendly website delivered +11.4% increase in easyJet.com conversion rate between 2011 and 2013.

CRM activity also proved highly effective in driving higher revenue per individual. By 2013, people in the marketable database were delivering 25% more revenue than those who weren't. Overall, this led to a 134% increase in annual financial contribution by marketing to £203 million in 2013, a return on investment of 6:1.

By 2013 that financial performance saw the company propelled into the FTSE 100 and deliver a record-breaking £478 million profit before tax (+51% YOY). The combination of all these factors contributed to an impressive period for the easyJet share price, which rose from 420p to 1,644p as of the 31st January 2014, leading to healthy dividends for shareholders.

All images appearing in this case study are reproduced by permission of easyJet.

AVIVA
Using new thinking to inspire brand loyalty

SNAPSHOT

Aviva employed a compelling campaign to give its intermediaries a reason to choose the brand at a time of unprecedented change in the market.

AGENCY

Teamspirit

KEY INSIGHTS

- The removal of adviser commission threatened one of Aviva's key channels because it meant that financial advisers who sold Aviva products had to find a way to communicate the value of financial advice most effectively.
- Aviva called on leading behavioural scientists to give the advisers persuasive arguments when they initiated conversations with their clients about the new regulations.
- The supportive materials supplied helped advisers to such an extent that key recommendation scores for Aviva rose dramatically against targets.

SUMMARY

Aviva is the UK's largest insurer and one of Europe's leading providers of life and general insurance, with a heritage stretching back over 300 years. It provides around 43 million customers with insurance, savings and investment products.

However, in 2012 the company faced a huge challenge. The government's Retail Distribution Review (RDR), which came into force at the end of that year, meant that financial advisers were no longer able to collect commission when recommending pensions and investment products – for many of them, their sole source of professional remuneration.

They would now need to convince clients to pay for advice or go out of business. After extensive research, Aviva launched a ground-breaking campaign to support those advisers who stayed in the industry where the need was greatest: to have more effective conversations about adviser charging with clients. This would differentiate the brand against bigger-spending competitors.

Aviva built its campaign with the help of two of the UK's leading behavioural scientists and produced tools for business survival, including a well-received book and videos. This created a strong bond with the brand and led to results which surpassed all targets, hopes and expectations.

FACING A MARKET UPHEAVAL

31 December 2012 marked the advent of the biggest single opportunity for Britain's UK financial advisers and the product providers who depended on them for sales. On that date, the government-led Retail Distribution Review (RDR) came into force, meaning that product providers could no longer pay commission to advisers for product sales. This transformed the distribution status quo that had existed for decades.

Overnight, fees from clients became the sole method of remuneration for financial advisers. This shifted the balance of power between brands and their adviser distributors forever in a number of ways:

- The adviser market would be much smaller. Many advisers had planned to quit the market post-RDR. Industry numbers had already shrunk from 37,000 to 20,000, so growing the importance of remaining advisers to product providers such as Aviva.
- Advisers' businesses would now survive based on the fees negotiated with their clients, the majority of whom had never paid their advisers a penny directly. Many clients would be reluctant to pay the fees and the required cost per hour. This was highlighted in Deloitte's white paper *Bridging the Advice Gap* which revealed that consumers would only be willing to pay under £70 an hour, while advisers needed £110-£150 per hour to cover their costs.
- Financial brands would now have massively increased importance at all stages of the customer journey, for advisers and consumers. With commission removed, sales would be based not only on the cost of advice but also the brand's credibility, recognition and quality.

What this meant was that business and marketing conventions that had succeeded for decades in this market no longer applied. A major part of Aviva's business was sales from advisers, representing a significant proportion of the UK life business's turnover. With all providers jostling for a shrinking adviser market, spending from competitors such as Standard Life, Scottish Widows and Prudential significantly increased, while Aviva's marketing budget remained level. This reduced its share of voice, and compromised its ability to influence advisers at what was a critical time.

In addition, although the strength of Aviva's relationship with advisers was now fundamental, a recent reallocation of sales territories meant that relationships between sales force and advisers were strained. Advisers found they had a new Aviva contact with whom they had no previous relationship. And while brand perceptions with consumers were high and positive, Aviva's brand relationship was far more inconsistent with advisers.

Aviva fully recognised that this was an important time for the industry. Brand relationships and business links forged now with advisers would have a lasting impact on Aviva's business for years to come.

It was time for new thinking. Aviva and Teamspirit, (the company's agency marketing partner of a decade) undertook a "root and branch" analysis of adviser activity.

UNCOVERING VALUABLE INSIGHTS
In early 2012, Aviva commissioned three pieces of research to generate insight along all stages of the customer journey and distribution chain, encompassing:
• **Advisers:** a new wave of its Adviser Brand Tracker (Figure 1).

Figure 1. Aviva Adviser Brand Tracker   Source: Aviva Adviser Barometer October 2012

- **Consumers:** research to probe understanding of the all-important changes to fee-based remuneration.
- **Aviva sales force:** quantitative research.

Aviva also commissioned painstaking analysis of competitor activity at marketing and business support level, since both were key dynamics for intermediary brand influence. This activity created the following insights that the subsequent 'New Thinking' campaign brought to life as a result.

- Fee conversations would be difficult. Consumers revealed a lack of knowledge about the fact that as of 31 December 2012 they would need to pay fees for advice that they had previously perceived as 'free'.
- Advisers were so busy planning for RDR that their time and interest for non-essential meetings with sales people would be low. This would obviously be a barrier to Aviva's sales force meeting with advisers at a critical time unless the conversation was of a high value.
- Profitability post-RDR was the most pressing adviser issue. Aviva research revealed that this was the most critical concern of 44% of those surveyed.
- Competitors' marketing activity around RDR was intense, but 'me-too' and short on practical content. Many had focused marketing support on similar topics: helping advisers define business models, understand new regulation and post-RDR customer remuneration. Yet Aviva and Teamspirit spotted a gap: there was a lack of support on the critical issue of influencing fee conversations.
- Aviva was seen as a strong consumer brand by advisers, but they questioned its ability to support small intermediary businesses innovatively post-RDR when they needed it most.

SETTING AMBITIOUS GOALS

Drawing on these insights, Aviva and Teamspirit devised an integrated communications plan with the following objectives.

1. Position Aviva as a practical business partner who understands the adviser's critical post-RDR business issues.
- Measures of success: positive shifts in perceptions from Aviva's Adviser Tracker against the measures 'Aviva is committed to supporting advisers' and 'Aviva provides me with practical business support'.

2. Start conversations with advisers from Aviva's sales force about Aviva's post-RDR product and service proposition.

• Measure of success: 300 new conversations between the sales force and advisers.

3. Generate an aggressive increase in Aviva's net promoter score (NPS) of 5% and an increase in 'likelihood to recommend Aviva' of 5%.

4. Generate engagement with advisers, via high levels of interaction with campaign materials.
• Measures of success:
  – 500 requests for the central element of the campaign, the proposed book on 'New Thinking'.
  – Targeted interactions with online materials and content: 4,000 web visits, two minutes online dwell time.

The timing of the campaign would be from October to the end of November 2012.

PUTTING IT ALL TOGETHER
There were a number of key elements to the campaign.

Creative strategy
Aviva and Teamspirit recognised that the most effective way to drive adviser influence was by increasing adviser profitability. This translated into helping advisers have a higher success rate in conversations about fees with clients. Cutting-edge influence in verbal and written communications was being achieved by behavioural scientists such as Professor Paul Dolan of the London School of Economics and best-selling business author Steve Martin. They had already been applying their thinking successfully in a variety of sectors, including the raising of an incremental £1 billion in revenues for local authorities through science-based phrasing and contextualising of messaging.

Despite their track record of consulting only on million-pound projects, Teamspirit persuaded both of these experts to take part in this campaign and conduct adviser research. A range of guides and videos were then produced with practical tips on how behavioural science could help advisers communicate the value of financial advice more persuasively.

Materials and initiatives included:
• **Book.** *New Thinking on Adviser Charging*. A 42-page guide was commissioned as the key content of the campaign. Written by Professor Dolan and Steve Martin, it applied behavioural science to the issue of charging fees, with practical tips on influencing clients (Figure 2).

• **Videos.** A series of films were created, presented by Dolan and Martin, which gave advisers tutorials on how to have more successful fee conversations using behavioural science (Figure 3).

Figure 2. *New Thinking on Adviser Charging* book

Figure 3. Fee conversation video tutorials

Figure 4. Sales aids

- **Sales aids.** A number of practical, downloadable sales aids were created showing how advisers could influence using key adviser channels: letters, emails, face-to-face and telephone (Figure 4).

Putting the Aviva sales force at the heart of the strategy.
Aviva's sales force were engaged in the campaign far earlier than usual, both to gain their insight into advisers' needs and give them co-ownership of the strategy and results. They were asked to select new and existing advisers that they wanted to start new sales conversations with. The commercial importance of this campaign was stressed through regular internal communications.

Media strategy
A media strategy was designed that used complementary media based on their particular strengths:

Figure 5. Aviva campaign online advertising

- Privileged pre-release of 'New Thinking' campaign content to targeted advisers. Advisers selected by the sales force were mailed advance information on the campaign, highlighting its business value and inviting requests for the New Thinking book.
- Rich media sampling and web traffic building. Crucial to the campaign's success was driving interactivity with campaign materials on Aviva's adviser website. Responsive rich media units were embedded with rich media footage, hinting at the high-value behavioural science films and materials that advisers would find on Aviva's website. (Figure 5)
- Thought leadership communications. Aviva sponsored the high profile Online *Financial Times* Adviser Surgery – and the opinion page – to achieve the moral high ground. Advertorials, public relations and industry events (such as the Institute of Financial Planning conference) were used to communicate how RDR necessitated new thinking on fees, with Aviva as the champion of the issue.
- Innovative trade press advertising. This was used to achieve media cut-through (Figure 6).

Figure 6. Trade press advertising

Internal communications
Regular communications with the sales force during the campaign maintained momentum, shared successes and used behavioural science principles to help Aviva's sales force have more successful conversations with their targeted advisers.

Regular campaign 'refreshing'
To keep campaign momentum and response rates high with a low media spend, the campaign updated the creative content three times in an eight-week period, which was far more regular than historically for Aviva campaigns.

MAKING A LASTING IMPRESSION
The results exceeded expectations on every front:

1. Significant outperformance on NPS against target. As a direct result of this campaign:
• Advisers were 15% more likely to recommend Aviva (target 5%).
• The brand saw its NPS achieve 31% higher than the target of 5% (Figure 7).

	Seen advertising	Not seen advertising
I feel very highly valued by Aviva	26%	8%
Aviva is the provider I would prefer to recommend	40%	25%
Net Promoter Score	10%	-21%

Those who have seen the advertisements were more likely to feel valued, more likely to recommend Aviva to others and more likely to give a positive Net Promoter Score than those who did not recall seeing advertising.

Figure 7. Net Promoter Score   Source: Aviva Brand Tracker

2. Post-campaign adviser brand metrics, for 'completely/very important' scores, were dramatically higher:
• 'Aviva provides me with practical business support'. There was an increase of 240% against the previous Brand Tracker wave.
• 'Aviva is committed to supporting advisers'. This saw an increase in 60% against the previous wave.

3. Key metrics of adviser interaction with campaign channels and materials were definitively surpassed:
• 'Top 10 bestselling business book'. The *New Thinking* book was requested by 5,004 advisers (or the equivalent of 54% of Aviva's 8,000 adviser partners), against an initial print run of 500. If the book had been sold, this would have ranked in the 'Top 10' non-fiction UK book chart.
• Over-achievement of campaign adviser web visits by 254% against an already aggressive target of 4,000.
• Interaction with *New Thinking* content on website 510% over target. Downloads of behavioural science top tips were over five times that of targets based on recent high-performing Aviva campaign benchmarks. Dwell time on the site was an average of 4.25 minutes.

4. There was notable over-delivery of campaign targets for new adviser conversations by an impressive 624% at an industry-critical time. Over 2,050 new conversations were started with the sales force as a direct result of the campaign.

5. Industry recognition. So successful was the campaign that the chief executive of the industry's independent trade body, the Institute of Financial Planning, Nick Cann commented: "The biggest change in financial services regulation means that in 2013 many advisers clearly need to think differently if they are to deliver the kind of service that their clients will happily pay fees for. What stands out to me about the 'New Thinking' campaign from Aviva is that it focuses on behavioural issues and gives financial planners relevant and practical help that they can apply immediately to their businesses. It is an innovative approach and shows that Aviva is a company that understands advisers' needs."

All images appearing in this case study are reproduced by permission of Aviva.

CHAPTER 3 03
Communicating brilliantly

Great marketing communications can both establish and transform a brand as few other marketing levers can. In my view there are five core principles that underpin great communication. These cases delivered against all five overall, but also individually illustrate each one of the principles particularly well.

Have something to say. McDonald's managed to find something relevant to say in spite of the almost impossible conundrum of associating fast food with sport – and not just any sport, but one of the biggest sporting events in the UK's calendar, Olympics 2012.

Understand your audience. John Lewis based its campaign on an insight that informed every aspect of its campaign: shoppers could clearly relate to the thoughtfulness of a well-chosen gift.

Use emotion to connect. Galaxy rediscovered the emotional attribute of its brand by getting away from 'guilty secrets' to the classy story of women who indulge and found the perfect icon in Audrey Hepburn.

Make your brand central to the story. Sainsbury's was well placed as a major food retailer to comment on the full range of attitudes to Christmas where food plays a central role and employed crowd-sourcing to spectacular effect.

Use creativity to achieve more than your budget implies is possible.
The multi-layered approach used by the MINI got the brand's passionate fans to create the content to help persuade reluctant car buyers that they weren't just paying for the badge.

Jan Gooding
Group Brand Director
Aviva

MCDONALD'S
Winning the audience over

SNAPSHOT

McDonald's successfully overcame initial criticism of its Olympic Games sponsorship with an imaginative campaign celebrating the general public's role in the event.

AGENCIES

Leo Burnett, OMD, The Marketing Store

KEY INSIGHTS

- McDonald's was being criticised for the inappropriateness of a fast-food brand associating with an event that celebrated sporting perfection.
- The campaign's vision of focusing on the pivotal role that the general public would play in setting the Games alight and the imaginative use of digital media significantly transformed the brand's standing.
- The results were increased brand affinity and positive word-of-mouth as well as a sales uplift.

SUMMARY

McDonald's is the world's leading food-service retailer, with more than 34,000 local restaurants serving nearly 69 million people in 118 countries each day. When the Olympic Games came to London in 2012, the company's prominent position in the market made it a natural sponsor of what was set to be one of the most exciting Olympic events in history.

Nevertheless, along with other sponsors, McDonald's came in for fierce criticism by those who felt certain brands were a bad fit with a sporting event, and who dubbed London 2012 'the obesity Games'. So the company and its agency, Leo Burnett, faced a big challenge: to drive affinity for the

McDonald's brand by making people feel good about its sponsorship of London 2012. Ultimately, the aim was to increase sales, as affinity is a proven sales driver.

The solution was to find common ground between a sponsor and an event seemingly poles apart by celebrating the values that London 2012 and McDonald's shared: democracy and generosity of spirit. It shifted the focus from athletes to the people, recognising that the Games are a special and inclusive event where everyone has a role to play.

Content was delivered to consumers in a fun way through different media and invited people to share it via digital channels. The campaign resulted in increases across all appropriateness and affinity measures and changed the conversation, reducing negative and increasing positive buzz. August 2012 saw McDonald's UK's biggest ever sales along with a healthy return on investment (ROI).

BRAND UNDER PRESSURE

Brand affinity is a proven sales driver for McDonald's, and the Games offered a prime opportunity to generate affinity on a global stage. London 2012 was McDonald's' ninth Games as 'official restaurant', and its first as the official presenting partner of the Games Makers, or all the volunteers who would actually help make the Games work. However, it presented what was probably the brand's toughest affinity challenge ever.

Health campaigners, politicians and media criticised sponsors that people felt were a bad fit with athletics. London 2012 was dubbed 'the obesity Games' and the London Assembly urged the International Olympic Committee to ban sponsorship of the Games by companies that produce high-calorie food and drink (Figure 1).

Figure 1. Spoof campaign

To make matters worse, McDonald's came under fire for exclusivity arrangements regarding the sale of chips in the Olympic Park. By July 2012, McDonald's was the sponsor with the highest awareness, but fewer than one in five people thought it was an appropriate sponsor. Similarly, McDonald's dominated online conversation compared to other Games sponsors, but over half of that chat was negative in sentiment.

Meanwhile, YouGov's brand index showed McDonald's net sentiment at -12.5, the lowest for two years. So, as the association of McDonald's with the Games became a hornet's nest of negativity and criticism, how could McDonald's' Olympic sponsorship be used to make people feel good about the brand?

FINDING THE RIGHT STORY TO TELL

McDonald's Olympic association goes back to 1968, when the company airlifted hamburgers to US athletes who were homesick for Big Macs. Since then, McDonald's had often highlighted its role in "feeding the Games", providing "athletes, coaches and officials with a familiar taste of home." However, the cultural climate of 2012 meant that the campaign couldn't focus on athletes. The solution would be to find shared territory with the Games.

The Olympics have long celebrated values such as excellence. But for London 2012 there was a new vision. As Lord Coe, chairman of the London Organising Committee of the Olympics and Paralympics Games (LOCOG), said in 2007: "London 2012 will be everyone's Games. This is the vision at the very heart of our brand. It's an invitation to take part and be involved."

McDonald's positioning is 'the people's restaurant', a place that is democratic and populist. From Olympic athletes to the man on the street, "There's a McDonald's for everyone". McDonald's had great Olympic stories to tell – from training the Games Makers to the champion crew. But research said that no story would drive affinity on its own.

So to make people feel good about the sponsorship, the company and its agency decided to highlight the things that people love about McDonald's, including inclusivity, democracy and generosity of spirit and show how these values were shared with London 2012.

To demonstrate these shared values, the discussion shifted the focus, from the athletes to the people and, in doing so, recognised an essential truth: that the Games were not just a demonstration of sporting excellence, but also a kind of carnival, a celebration of human endeavour that appealed to not just 'the fans', but people who do not ordinarily follow sports events.

People would be coming together to cheer on the world's athletes and would create an atmosphere of connection and euphoria on the streets. They would be warm hosts, welcoming the world and proudly showing them the best of their country and what it can achieve. The records would be broken in the stadiums, but the people would make the Games (Figure 2).

Figure 2. The people's Games

This was expressed in the line: 'We all make the Games':
• It was a rallying cry celebrating how the public, Games Makers and McDonald's crew would come together to make London 2012 the greatest show on earth.
• It was a unifying story that wrapped a range of McDonald's Olympic contributions into a coherent theme.
• It was refreshingly different. Many brands fell back on tired sporting analogies, giving the brand an opportunity to stand out.

For the first time, people would be capturing and sharing the Games as they happened. They would not just be watching it on TV or in a stadium, but actively participating in creating the narrative of the Games. This was an unbeatable opportunity to not just say, but really show, how 'We all make the Games.'

It was clear that this would be the first 'people's Games' in a real sense, because they would be the first Olympics where social media had come of age. McDonald's, as 'the people's restaurant' could support this behaviour. There was confidence that the brand could play this role, because, despite the criticism, consumer tracking showed a solid and increasing baseline of trust in and affinity for the brand.

Meanwhile, the Games were riding a wave of positivity: in 2007, just 7.5% of people thought that the Games would have a positive effect on people. By 2011, 27.9% thought so. And while there was plenty of pre-Games carping about logistics, that was seen as simply the British way to be pessimistic about what could go wrong. But the company and agency believed that once the 'home advantage' and an unprecedented celebratory context was added in (the Royal Wedding and the Golden Jubilee had brought the nation together, most notably in street parties, the like of which hadn't been seen since 1977) Britain was primed for a summer of saying "I was part of it".

CREATING A VIRTUOUS CIRCLE

This all led to the guiding principle of the campaign: the collective story of the Games would be celebrated in a way that would be alive and responsive and capture the mood of each moment as the Olympic story unfolded. This would show clearly that 'We all make the Games'.

The campaign wove a universe of touchpoints together (Figure 3):
1. **Celebrate.** The people behind the Games were celebrated with a launch TV commercial.
2. **Invite.** People were invited to share their Olympic content through digital channels, while live footage of their experiences was captured.
3. **Amplify.** People's Olympic content was fed back to them in fun, rewarding ways using a range of channels across different media, including two new TV commercials, to respond to what was happening during the Games.

Figure 3. Campaign touchpoints

1. Celebrate
The campaign launched two weeks before the opening ceremony to capitalise on the anticipation. The TV ad and a huge 48-sheet outdoor campaign introduced the idea of

'Olympic fan types': Games Makers, champion crew and fans experiencing the rollercoaster emotional ride of the Games in all kinds of ways. The commercial invited people to Facebook, asking "What kind of fan are you?" (Figures 4 and 5).

Figure 4. Olympic fan types

Figure 5. Olympic fan types

2. Invite
The call to get involved was echoed across multiple media, with placements next to relevant Games content. On Facebook, people used the Fanalyser app to share pictures of their Olympic experiences. 20,000 people from 39 different countries did so – a 60% conversion rate. But you didn't have to submit content to get involved: film crews were capturing Games moments as they happened at venues and fan parks.

3. Amplify
This film content fuelled four new TV ads from the Olympics and Paralympics, made up of live moments of real people experiencing the Games.
- For example, as Bradley Wiggins won his gold medal, 'The fake hair on cheekers' was introduced (Figure 6).
- Soon after Usain Bolt won the 100 metres, 'The 9.63ers' were showcased.
- As the Paralympics began, 'The inspired to try-ers' became the heroes.

Figure 6. "The fake hair on cheekers" TV ad

Figure 7. Outdoor campaign

Responsive TV was only the start. The pictures submitted through Facebook, and the footage from the film crews, became the basis of the digital outdoor campaign. Outdoor delivered both impact and frequency. It was the largest-ever live poster campaign to date, involving 250 digital posters and over 300 pieces of digital display. This was about using a large media spend innovatively to service the people's narrative, not simply to broadcast brand messaging (Figure 7).

THE MESSAGE COMES ALIVE

Dominating London transport hubs ensured that almost everyone arriving for the Games would see the celebrations of fellow fans. Special builds all included digital screens, with 3G Wi-Fi technology to enable live updates. Meanwhile, the rest of the country saw thousands of 48-sheets, using premium backlit formats to maximise impact. The ads included the name and home town of their star, ensuring that they didn't seem London-centric.

Back in London, the iconic McDonald's Piccadilly sign displayed the fans' submissions. The amplification linked back to small screens, with the people starring on all

McDonald's touchpoints, digital display, and an MSN homepage takeover seen by 4.7 million unique users. In addition, to make sure they didn't miss a thing, fans were told via Facebook when and where they would be appearing on the digital outdoor, with video clips showing their moment of fame (Figure 8).

A partnership with News International took 'We all make the Games' into people's hands with national institutions like *The Times* and *The Sun* celebrating Olympic fans' contributions to the Games. Across the entire 17 days, *The Sun* ran a co-branded double page spread showcasing the best pictures of how the public were 'making The Games', rewarding them with a moment of fame, and inviting others to get involved. Meanwhile, *The Times* reached opinion formers, telling the Games Makers' stories. Both papers placed campaign content alongside Games news, bringing the media and people's narratives together.

With the 'amplify' phase firing across social, broadcast and media platforms, the restaurants told a more detailed story.
- Photos of real Games Makers, champion crews, farmers and customers helped create a photographic mosaic that formed the silhouette of an Olympic crowd (Figure 9).
- A full window takeover was applied to 32 flagship restaurants, while window friezes, mobiles and tray liners highlighted the stories of the Games Makers, farmers and champion crews.
- Taking the message to the Olympic venues, press ads in the official programmes celebrated the Games Makers.

THE SULKY PANTS

WE ALL MAKE THE GAMES

Figure 8. Video clip

Figure 9. Games Makers mosaic

The campaign culminated in a TV commercial made entirely of footage captured during the Games, broadcast in the break after the Paralympics closing ceremony and celebrating the fact that 'We all made the Games'. It echoed the 'inspire a generation' ambition with new types of fans such as 'the future gold-getters'. Finally, a special Games Makers souvenir edition of *The Times* was created as a legacy, with copies given to all 70,000 of them.

WINNING RESULTS

The results proved that the campaign transformed the perception of the brand's fit with the Games.

1. Reduction in negative conversation about the brand.

There was a reduction in the negative conversations about the brand immediately after the main burst of media, reflecting its powerful cut-through in a very crowded context. The campaign achieved 77% standout compared to other Olympic advertising. McDonald's saw a significant increase in positive word-of-mouth offline compared especially to other sponsors.

2. Appropriateness and affinity.

People who were aware of the campaign were considerably more likely to believe that McDonald's was an appropriate sponsor and that the campaign went beyond this to make them actually feel good about it.

3. Commercial success.

August saw biggest-ever sales for McDonald's UK. 'We all make the Games' also achieved a significant sales impact despite the unusually tough context. Commercial viewing was down 22% due to the BBC Olympics coverage and communications awareness dropped for most brands tracked during this time, while retail sales in August were down by 0.4% on a like-for-like basis vs August 2011.

4. Return on investment (ROI).

The campaign delivered a healthy ROI. Although the econometric modelling showed a short-term ROI, it is believed that this is because it was an emotional, affinity-building campaign rather than a short-term sales driver so will continue to deliver a return on investment over the longer term. Long-term econometric models run by media analysis agencies consistently show ROIs that are at least 25.5 times higher than the short-term ROI, so it is estimated this campaign could deliver more over time.

All images appearing in this case study are reproduced by permission of McDonald's.

JOHN LEWIS
The power of emotions

SNAPSHOT

John Lewis has built on its acutely-observed marketing strategy emphasising deep human truths to become a modern retailing legend.

AGENCIES

adam&eveDDB, Manning Gottlieb OMD

KEY INSIGHTS

- In the midst of the economic downturn in 2009 retailer John Lewis realised that difficult times called for a radical rethink of its marketing strategy to compete as a mid-to-premium retailer.
- The result, an approach which centred on encouraging a much deeper emotional engagement between the brand and consumers, transformed the brand from one which was not only respected but to one which was loved, with sales from all departments reflecting its renewed fortunes.
- The multi-platform Christmas 2013 campaign was the culmination of this determination to engage with audiences across channels and achieved almost £9 profit for every £1 spent.

SUMMARY

It might be hard to recall, but in 2009 one of the UK's most-loved retailers was facing a challenging future. Like all its fellow retailers, John Lewis recognised the impending difficulties of the economic downturn, and as a mid-to-premium retailer this had the potential to be particularly acute. But there was more to it than this. John Lewis was trusted on many levels, but it wasn't loved. Research showed that this led to a low frequency of purchase and lower share of customer spend, as shoppers visited mainly for rational reasons, seeking products that they really needed to buy.

John Lewis decided to take a much more emotional communications approach to target people's hearts as well as their heads, and remind them there was so much at John Lewis to inspire and excite them. The first campaign was unveiled in Christmas 2009 and tapped into a new customer insight and product truth: John Lewis is the home of more thoughtful gifting because it has more products than any other department store and customers who are proud of the thought they put into selecting them as gifts.

This insight has formed the basis of all Christmas marketing activity for John Lewis ever since, including the 2013 'Bear & Hare' campaign. The power of emotional appeal was also applied to the retailer's underlying ethos of being 'Never knowingly undersold' and supported with such iconic campaigns as 'Always a Woman' that had the nation in tears.

This case study combines the winning entries from 2013 and 2014, and tells the story of a period when John Lewis recaptured its shoppers hearts and created marketing that has gone on to be a cultural phenomenon.

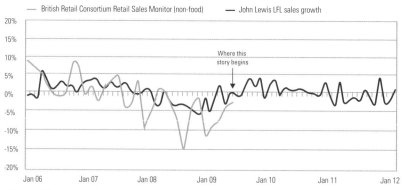

Figure 1. Sales growth (like-for-like) among UK non-food retailers vs. John Lewis prior to mid-2009

TRUSTED BUT NOT LOVED

By 2014 the UK retailer John Lewis was one of the most talked-about and admired advertisers in the UK. But, just a few years previously the retailer, like many of its high street counterparts, was suffering. For the previous 18 months prior to spring 2009, like-for-like sales had been negative and often more so than the British Retail Consortium's average (Figure 1).

The problem was that John Lewis as a brand faced a fundamental difficulty. Loyalty to department stores in general is driven most strongly by emotional affinity and perceived popularity, with rational affinity in third place and perceived price in fourth. However, tracking showed that John Lewis, while doing much better than expected in measures of rational affinity, given the size of the brand and compared to its competition, fared less well when it came to emotional dimensions and significantly worse than expected on perceived popularity and value. This underlined the challenge the retailer faced: it was trusted, but not loved.

This was affecting performance, with John Lewis suffering from low frequency of purchase and consequently low share of wallet among its key target customers. A new communications approach, with a more emotional appeal, to be developed with adam&eveDDB, was needed to achieve two objectives:
• The primary one was to encourage existing shoppers to visit and spend a little more.
• The secondary aim was to attract new shoppers.

CAPTURING THE CHRISTMAS SPIRIT

The first test of the new strategy would be Christmas 2009. The Christmas period is hugely important to John Lewis, since it accounts for around 40% of sales and 20% of profits. And a successful Christmas sets the business up well for the coming year, giving it great momentum and confidence. Rather than follow the usual seasonal advertising route of celebrities and sparkle, John Lewis chose to position itself as the

Figure 2. 'Remember the feeling' TV ad

home of a more thoughtful approach to gifts by celebrating those who put a lot of care into what they choose for others.

The resulting commercial, 'Remember the feeling', showed children unwrapping adult gifts with childish delight. It used a well-known track re-recorded by a contemporary artist, which was a model followed by all subsequent commercials (Figure 2).

The next three years built on this highly-emotional mood:
• The Christmas 2010 campaign was spearheaded by the TV ad 'For those who care'.
• 'The long wait' was created for Christmas 2011 and featured a young boy waiting to give a gift to his parents (and which reputedly caused a few parental tears to shed).
• In 2012 the snowman famously went on his' journey' accompanied by the plaintive tones of Gabrielle Aplin singing a new version of *The Power of Love*.

These campaigns all helped deliver market-leading commercial performance, and achieved a place in popular culture. They made the song charts in the top ten and even hit number 1, they generated millions of YouTube hits, won numerous polls as the UK's favourite ads, and, in the case of 'The long wait', became an official subject on the primary schools' teaching curriculum. But by Christmas 2013 the ambition was even bigger: to create the most integrated marketing campaign in its history by exploiting a broad multi-channel approach, including physical stores, online, mobile and the hybrid 'click and collect'.

THE BEAR AND HARE

The creative platform for the 2013 marketing campaign once again leveraged that truth of 'thoughtful gifting': give someone a Christmas they'll never forget. It focused on the creative idea of the joy of experiencing Christmas for the first time, seen through the eyes of someone who had always missed out: a hibernating bear.

The result, the story of 'the bear and the hare', was a captivating woodland tale of friendship between two animated characters (Figure 3). The bear always missed the fun and joy of Christmas because he hibernated through the winter. But this year his friend was determined to find a gift that would help him be part of the festivities: the gift of Christmas itself.

Figure 3. The 'Bear and Hare' ad

The TV ad was created using an advanced animation technique which blended three-dimensional sets with two-dimensional character drawings by Disney legend Aaron Blaise, the director of *Brother Bear,* who had also worked on *The Lion King* and *Pocahontas.*

It resulted in two minutes of beautifully-crafted animation which became the focal point of a comprehensive brand strategy which encompassed a wide range of platforms.

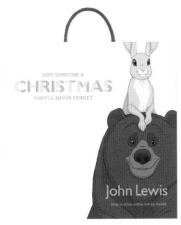

Figure 4. Carrier bags

- **In the stores.** The 'Bear and Hare' campaign theme was on every carrier bag (Figure 4). The characters themselves came to life in store with an interactive bear's cave which allowed children to hear the narrated version of the story and play interactive games. It also included a Brighton Pier-inspired woodland setting where children and adults could have their photo taken with woodland creatures.
- **In the shop window.** Each branch featured a bespoke 'Bear and Hare' window giving directions to the bear cave (Figure 5).
- **Merchandise.** A significant range of merchandise was sourced and sold in stores and online. This is the first time John Lewis has created such a range to activate a marketing campaign. It included alarm clocks, soft toys, hardback story books, pyjamas and onesies in all sizes. It had a 97% sell-through rate, with most of the range selling out within 10 days of campaign launch.
- **Online.** A bespoke app was created. The story of two friends was narrated by Lauren Laverne, with games and learning activities embedded in it. Over 300,000 downloads followed, while it topped Apple's leisure app chart. In addition, an online Christmas card-maker was developed which enabled customers to blend

Figure 5. Shop windows

themselves in with the woodland creatures to make cards for family and friends. Over 12,000 were created.

- **Social media.** Bespoke Twitter @handles were developed for the campaign's main characters. It resulted in 168 million impressions of #bearandhare and #sleepingbear in the opening weekend from 26,000 tweets. Through Twitter and social listening the retailer rewarded members of the public who had invoked the spirit of the story by going the extra mile with a framed limited edition print from the animation. Meanwhile, the Shazam music recognition app was taken over to reach all the people searching for the campaign music and it became the most 'Shazam'd'ad of 2013. Finally, a major competition – Reworked – ran on YouTube, inviting people to record their own version of the song. The winner, a busker from Liverpool, was rewarded by having his version, chosen by the song's original singer Keane, played in the Christmas Day ad.

- **Corporate social responsibility (CSR).** 'Bringing Skills to Life' is a free online primary school education programme created by John Lewis. 'Bear and Hare' activity cards were available to download for all three key primary age groups.

- Schools could then upload their pupils' work to an online gallery. Over 3,000 teachers visited that section of the site, with over 1,000 downloads of activity cards.

THINKING RADICALLY ABOUT MEDIA

The media plan for the 'Bear and Hare' campaign departed from the previous campaigns, which had positioned TV as the centrepiece of the plan. Now TV would be just one aspect of a comprehensive three-phase strategy:

Figure 6. Teaser ads

1. Tease. Working with ITV, John Lewis ran 10-second teasers with a mysterious hashtag #sleeping bear (Figure 6). The teaser 'ads' also carried a call to action to tune in to that Saturday's *X Factor* where all would be revealed. The teasers purposely de-branded and carried the station's logo to give the impression that ITV was launching something big in the show. About 4,000 tweets produced eight million impressions of the unbranded campaign hashtag, with Twitter opinion split between this being something to do with either John Lewis or Coca Cola.

At the same time, a special outdoor installation – a tree projection – was unveiled outside ITV's studios on London's South Bank. Unbranded, it encouraged people to tune in to the *X Factor* launch spot and also attracted tweets.

2. Launch. The ad was launched online first to allow customers and followers of John Lewis the chance to see it before it was broadcast nationally on TV. This generated further buzz, with 1.5 million people viewing it online before a single spot had aired on TV. Significantly, John Lewis had the first-ever takeover of a commercial break in the *X Factor* on the second Saturday in November, the show that is used by dozens of brands to launch their fight for most-loved Christmas TV ad.

3. Engage. The focus now switched to extending the story. Highlights included:
- 100% share of voice of Lily Allen's cover version in the Shazam music recognition app, so that when people Shazam'd the ad track they would be prompted to download the e-book as well.
- Ads in Apple and Android apps were run to promote the free e-book.
- Cinema goers were treated to the full-length two-minute ad (it had only been shown once before in the launch premiere break).
- Skippable ads were rolled out across video-on-demand to give viewers the option to watch the full-length ad rather than pushing it to them.

A HUGE CULTURAL AND COMMERCIAL IMPACT

The online response to the 2013 Christmas marketing campaign was overwhelming. The ad trended globally on Twitter within two hours of airing, while it was the most shared video in the world in November. Across the Christmas period it received 12.2 million YouTube views. This is actually 50% more people than tuned into the BBC's top-rated programme on Christmas Day, *Dr Who*, which averaged an 8.3 million audience.

Other significant activity included:
- An uplift in tweets of 21% compared to *X Factor* tweets when the ad broke on ITV. 4,000 tweets produced eight million impressions of the unbranded 'sleepingbear' hashtag.
- 500 entries were received for the YouTube soundtrack cover competition.
- 12,000 'Bear and Hare' online Christmas cards were sent by customers to friends and family.
- 300,000 'Bear and Hare' story apps were downloaded onto smartphones and tablets.
- 130,000 Shazams of Lily Allen's cover version.

Commercially, John Lewis was the clear winner across the key Christmas retail period in 2013. As well as out-performing its rivals and other big retailers, John Lewis also far outdid the overall retail average in like-for-like performance, as measured by the British Retail Consortium (BRC): 6.9% vs 0.4%.

Working with econometricians at Marketshare the company estimated that the campaign drove £128.4 million in incremental revenue, representing a revenue return on investment of £25.68, with a 10% uplift in profit ROI compared to 2012.

BUILDING ON THE BRAND PHILOSOPHY OF 'NEVER KNOWINGLY UNDERSOLD'

This has been the retailer's abiding ethos since introduced by founder John Spedan Lewis in 1925. While he had always meant it to be the very bedrock of the company's culture, it had, over the years, become just a price promise. As the recession continued it was felt that the time was right to return to the broader meaning of 'Never knowingly undersold' and put it back at the heart of the brand and encompass quality and service as well as price.

The new approach was encapsulated in 2010 with the commercial 'Always a woman' to demonstrate the constancy of John Lewis throughout key moments of a customer's life. This was followed by the 'Through the ages' campaign in the autumn of 2011, which continued the focus on the passage of time and the emphasis on 'Never knowingly undersold', but this time with technology and music as the source of emotional appeal. Then, in 2012 came 'The other half' which reminded customers that the important things in life never change, including the brand promise.

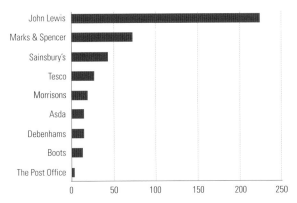

Figure 7. Newspaper coverage

BECOMING PART OF POPULAR CULTURE

All the John Lewis ads have been frequently discussed in the media, ensuring that a limited budget has gone much further than the actual recorded expenditure. For example, the Lily Allen soundtrack from Christmas 2013 went to number one for three weeks on the official UK charts, selling over 20,000 units, equating to a donation of more than £18,000 to the charity Save the Children. Every national newspaper covered the campaign, with over 200 articles in total (Figure 7). That included receiving the ultimate accolade: a spoof cover on the UK's prime satirical magazine, *Private Eye* (Figure 8).

Figure 8. *Private Eye*

Previous years' ads had also broken through into public consciousness. The ad 'Always a woman' was even the subject of BBC Radio 4's 'Thought for the Day' contribution as well as an exam topic for AS media studies, while 'The long wait' became an official subject for church sermons and school assemblies. Over 7,000 schools, encompassing over a million pupils, downloaded an assembly guide devoted to the ad.

The music from those ads has also been an important part of the advertising's entry into popular culture. The tracks have reached the charts and featured heavily in radio airplay. In 2012 the soundtrack for 'The journey' topped the official UK charts. The advertising value equivalent of this airplay and single downloads has been calculated to be worth over £15 million. This free coverage almost doubled the TV media investment.

PERFORMANCE 2009-2012

Looking back over the whole period, the retailer's decision to overhaul its communications strategy from 2009 onwards was transformative for the company's fortunes. Penetration, frequency and the average spend per customer showed marked increases. For example, tracking among customers in catchment areas showed that the ads significantly boosted the percentages of people who agreed that the ads 'made the brand more appealing' and that they made them 'more likely to shop at John Lewis'.

This translated into the primary objective: encouraging existing shoppers to visit and spend more, and the secondary objective of increasing penetration. Even more significantly, the company returned to growth after a difficult 2008. Between 2009 and 2012, the communications delivered £261 million in incremental profit, meaning that for every £1 spent £5.02 returned to the business.

An additional benefit has been the dramatic increase in the desirability of the brand to other suppliers, particularly those with premium brands, while further evidence of the increased commitment to John Lewis is the greater willingness of suppliers to contribute to funding the advertising.

Finally, there has been the impact on employee satisfaction and happiness. The overall stated purpose of the John Lewis Partnership is "the happiness of all its members, through their worthwhile and satisfying employment in a successful business". The communications have played a big role in fulfilling this objective, not only by giving them advertising they have enjoyed and felt proud of, but also by increasing the size of their annual bonuses.

All images appearing in this case study are reproduced by permission of John Lewis.

SAINSBURY'S
Crowd-sourcing creativity

SNAPSHOT

Sainsbury's rewrote the rules of retailer Christmas advertising with a campaign centred around a crowd-sourced film that resulted in one of the best trading weeks ever.

AGENCIES

AMVBBDO, PHD, Blue Rubicon

KEY INSIGHTS

- Sainsbury's made the bold decision to move from price-based Christmas advertising and use the emotional power of the brand to bring in customers and deliver growth.
- Thinking like a publisher led to the creation of a well-received 'day-in-the-life' film orchestrated by an Oscar-winning director using footage submitted by the public.
- A carefully-seeded media campaign across traditional and social platforms saw the retailer enjoy its 36th consecutive quarter of like-for-like sales growth.

SUMMARY

Sainsbury's is one the of the UK's leading retailers. Founded in 1869, it now has over 1,100 supermarkets and convenience stores and an online grocery and general merchandise operation, along with other interests.

Because the Christmas season is such a key battleground for supermarkets in terms of both sales and advertising, Sainsbury's started planning its strategy for Christmas 2013 well over a year ahead. Rather than put the focus on price, however, which was the usual route taken by an industry known for its short-term outlook, it bravely decided to put the creativity of the public at the heart of its communications.

The result was a campaign grounded in emotion, which used powerful content to create emotional engagement with the brand. It was built around an Oscar-winning director hired to capture how Britain really celebrates Christmas by using footage filmed and submitted by the public. This generated 20,000 clips, providing a fascinating insight into what UK families do during the holidays.

The film was launched just under a month before Christmas, following a two-week campaign on a number of platforms, including social media and television. It was a great success, leading to what Sainsbury's chief executive called the 'busiest ever' trading week before Christmas and helping to generate the 36th consecutive quarter of growth.

GEARING UP FOR THE MOST COMPETITIVE CHRISTMAS EVER

In 2013 supermarkets were facing one of the most competitive seasons ever. Years of total category growth were coming to an end while aggressive new competition had arrived from Waitrose, Lidl and Aldi. And, although it was tempting to see Aldi as a plucky underdog, during 2013 it had spent more on media than Sainsbury's.

As a result, the battle was even tougher among the 75% of the market accounted for by the 'big four' supermarkets. The perennial rivals (Tesco, Morrison's and Asda) had outspent Sainsbury's all year, a trend expected to continue at Christmas.

The assumption was that the three other competitors would spend most of their money on price and deals, as they had all year. In sharp contrast, Sainsbury's decided to take a brand-led approach.

This was a point of conviction, not necessity. After all, through the retailer's initiative called 'brand match', Sainsbury's customers would benefit from competitors' prices and deals anyway, so a compelling price/promotions story could have easily been told if desired. This contrasted with Waitrose, whose price position and relatively small number of promotions meant it couldn't really choose this route.

But Sainsbury's decided that rather than try and outspend the competition it would outsmart it. This called for thinking more like a publisher and using content to create emotional engagement with the brand. The retailer briefed its agency, AMVBBDO, to come up with an idea that would:
• Break the mould of supermarket advertising.
• Be so compelling that people would want to spend time with the brand, which would trigger greater awareness through earned media.

• Demonstrate that Sainsbury's understood the British Christmas better than anyone else, which would ultimately be reflected in sales.

Planning began some fifteen months before launch. Some of this strategic thinking fuelled the successful 2012 Christmas campaign, but the real focus was on preparing for the following year.

THE REAL MEANING OF THE HOLIDAY

The critical insight was what really matters at Christmas beneath the glitz and the glitter: the simple pleasures such as eating, drinking and being together. There was a close relationship between this and the retailer's well-known 'live well for less' ethos: both were about appreciating the small things and making the most of what you have. That insight could thus be used to demonstrate that Sainsbury's had a better understanding of Christmas than the competitors in terms of what 'living well for less' meant for customers.

To exploit the growth in video viewing AMVBBDO recommended long-form video content as the best way to capture the essence of the campaign. Oscar-winning director Kevin Macdonald was commissioned to capture the raw authenticity of how Britain really celebrated Christmas using footage filmed and submitted by the public.

Figure 1. Life in a Day

Figure 2. Kevin Macdonald

He had already demonstrated his expertise in making films with subtle but strong emotional appeal with *Life in a Day,* a 2011 crowd-sourced drama/documentary based on a series of video clips showing events in a single day in July 2010 (Figure 1).

Figure 3. Christmas in a day campaign   Figure 4. Clips from film

Kevin used YouTube to invite people to film their Christmas and share it with him (Figure 2). He was given total creative freedom to create the film he wanted, and an enthusiastic audience response generated 20,000 clips, totalling over 360 hours of footage. The film, produced by Scott Free Productions and Ridley Scott Associates, was a fascinating insight into how families across the country celebrated Christmas (Figure 3).

As well as ordinary images of traditional British celebrations, it included unsentimental moments from people who disliked the holiday or habitually ignored it for religious reasons, as well as breathtaking Christmas moments like the birth of child and a soldier's surprise family reunion (Figure 4).

A CAREFULLY-TIMED MEDIA STRATEGY

The campaign began by building anticipation with a launch of the campaign to Sainsbury's fans on Facebook and Twitter as well as an article in *The Daily Mail* online. Agency Blue Rubicon managed relationships with the real-life contributors to the film, as well as briefing influential retail and marketing correspondents with exclusive screenings, seen as critical to generating positive coverage and endorsement. When the ad actually launched on the 13th November there was editorial coverage in all the national newspapers.

The paid-for element of the campaign then kicked off with a 3.5-minute spot planned by PHD and which took up the entire *Coronation Street* break. Within five minutes #ChristmasInaDay was trending on Twitter.

The film launched on the 29th of November, two weeks after the campaign had gone live with paid support on key UK websites and outdoor positions. Different stories were then released at appropriate times to keep the momentum going in the run-up to Christmas day. For example:
- On December 2nd, broad coverage of the film in national press drove film views.
- On the 5th, a number of industry polls created hype around the film in advertising and arts circles.
- On the morning of the 8th a promoted Twitter trend ran, asking people to guess what happened next in the film. The winners won Sainsbury's vouchers.
- That evening, the 3.5 minute trailer took over the *X Factor* ad break. *X Factor* also tweeted from its Twitter handle.
- On Christmas Eve people were encouraged to watch the film with their families.
- Christmas Day saw the ad released with a Merry Christmas message.

During the campaign film clips were released at topical and relevant moments, such as:
- The 40" 'Christmas Tree' launched earlier in the season when customers were thinking about putting up decorations.
- The 60" 'Dancing' clip appeared later when the festive season was in full swing.

Characters in the trailers caught the nation's imagination. For example, the surprise return of the army dad from Afghanistan had the nation in tears, while the 'Spreadsheet Guy' became an internet star, with people desperate to get hold of his festive spreadsheet for the perfect turkey lunch.

BRAND POWER
The film was successful enough to be compared to other movies rather than ads, since 48 minutes is a much greater investment of time than watching a 60" or 90" ad. Interestingly, had it been a theatrical release, it would have been placed in fifth place in movie admissions in December, placing it ahead of *Gravity, The Secret Life of Walter Mitty* and *Saving Mr Banks*.

The campaign also had a high profile on social media and on other editorial platforms:
- More than three million views of 'Christmas in a Day' content on YouTube.
- An 11.5 million reach for the social conversations that were generated in the week after launch.
- 92% of conversations were positive.
- £1.9 million worth of PR value was generated, with 235 pieces of coverage spanning national, regional, trade, specialist film and arts media.

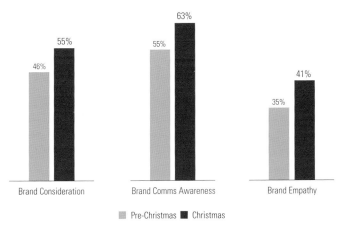

Figure 5. Key brand tracking measures   Source: HPI Brand Tracking

- Influential organisations such as Mumsnet and celebrities like Cheryl Cole took to Twitter about it.
- There was coverage in programmes like the *BBC's Newsnight*, ITV's *Daybreak* and *8 out of 10 Cats*.
- It was voted number one Christmas ad by readers of *Campaign* and *Ad Age* (74% and 55% respectively).

Similarly, brand measures reflected the impact of the campaign (Figure 5).
- Brand consideration during the period the campaign was live rose from 46% to 55% – a large rise for such a mature brand.
- Brand communications awareness during the Christmas period was 63% (second in the market). This was +8% vs. 2012 with flat media spend and a consistent share of voice.
- The campaign drove a +6pt increase in brand empathy from 35% to 41%. This opened up clear blue water between Sainsbury's and Tesco, which finished with 34%.

Other measures underlined the campaign's strong performance:
- It scored 68% on HPI's 'standout' measure, making it a top two ad since tracking began (in line with Sainsbury's Paralympic campaign in 2012).
- 'Likeability' of 69% (total sample), 85% (among the core target of mums) made it the most-liked supermarket Christmas ad since tracking began.
- Of all the retail Christmas campaigns, Sainsbury's was spontaneously judged to have the most influence on where people intended to shop.

DEFYING THE ODDS

Significantly, Sainsbury's defied analysts' predictions and posted 0.2% growth in the 14 weeks running up to Christmas. This was the latest in a remarkable run of like-for-like sales growth that had continued for the 36th consecutive quarter. And it was in a market where even the top performing players had to sprint just to stand still amid growing threats at both ends of the value spectrum.

But those figures by no means told the whole story. The real impact could be seen from the Kantar data that compared all the supermarkets in the last six weeks of the year, when the fight for Christmas was really on (Figure 6).

Figure 6. Kantar results

Measuring from the 12th of November through Christmas when the campaign was running, Sainsbury's outperformed the total market ahead of even Waitrose's +4.1% growth. Aldi grew by 28.2%, but this was seen as unsurprising, considering its 12% share of voice (the same as Sainsbury's) which was three times its 4% share of market (Sainsbury's share is 17.7%). Also note that for every £1 Sainsbury's spent on Christmas media in 2013, Tesco spent £1.67, Asda £1.62 and Morrison's £1.30.

Sainsbury's then-chief executive Justin King proclaimed it the "best Christmas ever" and the seven days before Christmas as the retailer's "busiest ever" trading week, with over 28 million transactions. The campaign not only drove millions more in incremental sales, but the return on investment was reckoned to have fully justified the content-based approach.

All images appearing in this case study are reproduced by permission of Sainsbury's.

MINI
Mining a rich seam of brand passion

SNAPSHOT

MINI's 'Not Normal' social media campaign worked to get non-owners to understand why the brand attracted such passionate fans – and saw a pronounced uplift in brand perception and consideration as a result.

AGENCY

iris

KEY INSIGHTS

- Despite MINI's place in the pantheon of British icons, too many potential buyers were proving reluctant to pay a premium simply 'for the badge'.
- An engaging social media campaign was built around the creativity and enthusiasm of MINI fans with the aim of educating the doubters of both the emotional and rational benefits of the brand.
- The 'Not Normal' campaign transformed brand perception among those in the market for a small car, with more than a third convinced that the MINI was worth the investment.

SUMMARY

The MINI, an iconic small car originally developed in the UK back in 1959, came to be seen as one of the emblems of 'swinging London' in the 1960s. Now owned by BMW, the MINI still arouses as much fervour and attachment in its owners as it did back then. However, there had been growing concern that too many irreverent ads meant that people who were in the market for a small car were starting to think that the MINI's quirky personality was unnecessary and, even worse, in some cases superficial. In a category where practicality counted more than ever, the MINI's strong brand was beginning to get in the way of its benefits.

In tackling this, in addition to addressing the awareness of the product benefits, it would be critical not to lose sight of an important brand truth: that the MINI is a car that inspires passion and creativity like few other cars. Those who drive MINIs aren't just owners. They are fans.

Communicating that would be a challenge to those who weren't already in love with the brand. Rather than try and get the message across in a traditional ad, social media and innovative out-of-home became the focal point for the 'Not Normal' campaign. Its humour and creativity resulted in marked rises in a range of key brand measures, including a 36% increase in the perception of the MINI as being worth a bigger investment.

MAKING A STRATEGIC ASSESSMENT

Since the MINI had been relaunched in 2001, the small car category had been through a revolution. Repeated new launches from the Audi A1 to the Fiat 500 and Vauxhall Adam meant that every major car marque had its own model of a small, fun car with a big personality and big budgets to match. The MINI, once a byword for the category, was facing an ever-increasing threat.

Meanwhile, the brand's own expanding range and ambitious growth targets had driven a need to create a new generation of MINI fans. Having accelerated to 2.6% of the total car market during its first decade since the UK relaunch, the brand had to reach outside its core fan base and help new audiences discover what made being a MINI owner so compelling.

There were four key objectives:
• Drive brand preference.
• Drive brand consideration.
• Drive purchase intent.
• Drive recommendation.

The MINI is a premium product and price was proving to be a key barrier to purchase. Qualitative research supported the hypothesis that many chose not to buy a MINI because they believed they were simply 'paying for the badge'. Although that premium stemmed from the brand's world-class design, build and performance, because those target groups currently didn't see enough difference between the MINI and the competition, they went for the cheaper, 'good enough' options.

To overcome those barriers and bring more people into the world of the MINI, the task was to encourage the audience to understand just how different a MINI really was. They needed to be helped to appreciate that by settling for a cheaper, less interesting alternative they were undermining the quality of their whole driving experience.

The greatest spenders in the category, Fiat 500, VW Golf and Citroen DS3, had been pouring up to three times MINI's budget on a variety of big campaigns in the same period, from mass awareness drives to spectacular stunts. MINI needed to punch higher to create a real cultural impact.

And that meant entering the age of social media. The brand that made its name in the Noughties by putting cars on the sides of buildings had to reconnect with people on a more human level by playing to its strengths of heritage and provenance, its iconic products and the passion of the people who drove them. This would be the way to increase consideration, preference and purchase intent for the brand significantly.

Care had to be taken, however. Times had changed since the MINI's quirky personality first relaunched onto the scene in 2001. The car-buying process had become increasingly functional and rational. Much of the target audience had started to see the MINI's irreverence as unnecessary. In a category where practicality counted, the MINI's brand could get in the way of its benefits.

GETTING TO THE HEART OF THE MATTER
Talk to any of the 1,250 drivers who joined the annual MINI pilgrimage from London to Brighton and it was clear that those penny-pinching VW Golf drivers were missing the point. The MINI's special combination of design, performance and history inspired a passion and creativity like no other. MINIs didn't have owners — they had fans.

To stop those Golf buyers taking the 'safe' option and giving them the confidence to invest in a MINI meant helping them reassess the very role of a car in their lives, turning what had become an increasingly rational purchase back into an emotional one. They needed to be reminded that a car should be something they had a relationship with.

But it would be difficult to convince the cynics through an ad that trumpeted how they were missing out. Instead, the communications had to get this audience to experience the emotions and passion of current MINI owners so they could see for themselves. The next stage was to delve more deeply into MINI relationships by listening to social media comments and holding face-to-face conversations with these owners.

They fell into four categories:

- Obsessive fandom. This included those MINI fanatics who defined themselves by their passion for the car through actions as extreme as tattooing themselves with a MINI.
- Product participation. This was about the everyday high jinks involving the car that anyone with a MINI could have a go at, such as: how many people can you fit into a MINI?
- Inventive tributes. This encompassed those creative types looking to express themselves through the medium of a MINI, echoing the iconic design in anything from cakes to moss.
- Cultural moments. This was about the MINI fuelling particularly British social occasions, like the couple who got married in their MINI.

The scale and diversity of those creative, charming tributes inspired by the MINI went beyond that of any other car brand. And the more stories that were unearthed about the time, effort and passion that people put into each of these creations, one thing became clear: the relationship MINI owners have with their cars is different from any other. It is creative, it is inventive and, above all, it is not normal (Figure 1).

This was a rich insight that, if expressed in the right way, would soften the heart of even the most resolute Golf driver towards the MINI brand. But this had to be treated carefully as any degree of advertising artifice could easily dissolve the simple charm unearthed in those tributes from the fans.

Figure 1. MINI cake

WELCOME TO THE WORLD OF MINI

The plan was to help the target audience discover these tributes naturally, accidentally and authentically. So the advertising message would be kept to a minimum and these discoveries would be shared in the simplest way possible, based on a number of key principles:

1. **Invite participation.** The 'Not Normal' campaign launched with a 30-second 'call to arms' film to get the whole country involved in shooting and sharing their own creations. In the spirit of social openness, the audience were allowed to contribute their creations any way they liked, from Twitter to Instagram to Vine, as long as they tagged it #MININotnormal (Figure 2).

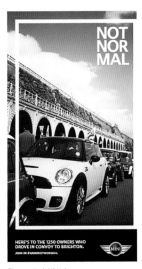

Figure 2. 'Furry' MINI   Figure 3. MINI fans

2. **Keep it real.** There would be no slick car photography, no lifestyle shots and no product benefits. These expressions of MINI passion would simply be allowed to surface in as straightforward a way as possible. The 'Not Normal' visual device became a consistent visual identity across a range of consumer content, from films and vines to illustrations and amateur photography. The tributes themselves had the starring role, while the creator was saluted with a unifying 'here's to' followed by their real name or social user ID (Figure 3).

3. **More is more.** The sheer volume and diversity of MINI tributes was what was most powerful. Bringing just one or two to the fore would seem contrived. Instead, the audience had to be helped to discover as many as possible to appreciate the passion inhabiting the world of the MINI. A 100% digital out-of-home (OOH)

strategy would involve sharing 'Not Normal' content in real time across every connected poster site it was possible to get hold of. No two posters would be the same, with new social content uploaded every day throughout the campaign.

4. **Urgent genius.** For the campaign to feel like a living, breathing part of the culture, it needed to happen at the speed of the culture itself. An 'always-on' team of copywriters and designers worked with the social monitoring team aggregating the content to create individual pieces of MINI-based content at a rate of up to 20 a day for six weeks (Figures 4 and 5).

5. **A picture is worth a thousand words.** In the modern social web, images are the ultimate social currency. This was at its heart a visual campaign, capitalising on the power of creative imagery to tell a brand narrative. But to really understand the MINI difference, the target audience would need to unearth the full story behind these 'Not Normal' relationships. That led to an advertising partnership with Buzzfeed with a wider public relations (PR) campaign to provide a back story behind the images.

Along with showcasing and paying tribute to the MINI owners' passions, it was critical that the MINI proved itself just as creative and passionate a participant in that relationship. So, three weeks in, the campaign took a surprising twist in honour of the tradition of the MINI 'salute', where MINI owners greet each other with a flash of their

Figure 4. 'Green fingers' MINI

Figure 5. MINI as a sandcastle

headlights. Anyone driving a MINI down London's busy Cromwell Road would be greeted with a 'Not Normal' salute shared across five giant digital posters.

By combining a bespoke technical platform and specially-trained spotters, messages were tailored to the make and colour of the passing MINI. Drivers were encouraged to participate with the message and were rewarded for interacting with treats such as a free car wash, free petrol or flowers.

News of this quickly spread across the social landscape and owners went out of their way to experience their own MINI 'thank you'. In just one week, the sites personally saluted 1,942 individual drivers.

BRAND IMPACT
The campaign was built to allow different types of consumers to interact in different ways: from skimming the surface, to those wanting to know more, to those who wanted to get fully involved. Over the course of those six weeks the numbers involved in all three forms of interaction were substantial.

1. Those who skimmed the surface:
- 230,000 engaged with the core campaign via social media by sharing, liking, commenting and viewing the streams of 'Not Normal' content.
- 50,000 shared the Cromwell Road films.
- 85,000 engaged with the Buzzfeed partnership.

2. Those who wanted to know more:
- 74,356 visited the campaign hub page to dive into the 'Not Normal' story.
- 29,181 new fans were acquired on Facebook.
- There was between 9.8% – 14.2% virality of Facebook posts.

3. Those who wanted to get fully involved:
- 2,217 shared their own content.
- 1,942 owners interacted with the Cromwell Road posters.

An integrated campaign evaluation (ICE) study was conducted by the Vizeum Insight team with a nationally-representative sample of 80% of the target audience, ABC1 25-55 year-olds in the market for a small car. The key measures were the shift in the three key objectives:

- 27% uplift in consideration.
- 33% increase in brand preference.
- 44% rise in purchase intent.

Meanwhile, specific scores for 'MINI is appealing' and 'MINI is like a friend' rose 18%.

40% of the total budget was dedicated to a global TV commercial that ran at the same time as the core social campaign. However, econometric modelling in the ICE tracker isolated the impact of this social campaign in driving the shifts in the brand performance. The findings showed that the digital OOH campaign, including the 'Thank you' stunt, accounted for 71% of the total shift in brand perception but only 27% of the spend.

Most notably, content shared through social media was three times more efficient at driving those measures, while 11% of the total campaign impact came from the synergy of those seeing both the digital OOH and the social media. In total, the core social campaign was identified as being responsible for over 90% of those shifts in brand scores.

And, although the campaign wasn't built to be directly lead-generating, of the participants who visited the campaign hub, 3,593 went on to look at a MINI for themselves at MINI.co.uk. 10% of those went on to become qualified dealer leads, while the dealerships themselves got involved in the campaign and started creating their own 'Not Normal' events and stunts, extending the life of the idea even further.

The campaign accounted for an uplift of 36% against the perception that the 'MINI is worth what it costs'. And, more importantly, the 'Not Normal' campaign succeeded in creating a new generation of lifelong MINI fans.

All images appearing in this case study are reproduced by permission of MINI.

GALAXY
Finding the brand's sweet spot

SNAPSHOT

A memorable communications campaign based on the brand's strong heritage and personified by an iconic Hollywood star relaunched the GALAXY® chocolate brand.

AGENCY

AMVBBDO

KEY INSIGHTS

- One of the most important brands in the Mars chocolate portfolio, Galaxy, had wanted to reconnect to its heritage of elegance and sophistication.
- Careful analysis of the brand's history led to its repositioning as a more refined, sophisticated pleasure and was brought to life through the ultimate 'Galaxy girl', Audrey Hepburn.
- Resurrecting the iconic star revitalised the brand's true personality and re-invigorated the brand.

SUMMARY

Mars is one of the world's leading consumer goods companies, with net sales of more than $33 billion and with business segments including chocolate, food, drinks and petcare. Launched in 1960 in the UK, Galaxy had long been one of the UK's favourite chocolate brands, renowned for its silky smooth taste and memorable advertising.

More recently, the brand had strayed from its heritage. A new communications campaign was aimed at recapturing the brand's spirit and bringing it firmly into the 21st century, restoring its iconic status. Research led Galaxy to be positioned as a more refined, sophisticated pleasure, an idea brought to life through another icon of the 20th century, Audrey Hepburn. She featured in an elegant film which used state-of-the-art techniques to tell a story of female confidence and ingenuity set in the 1950s on Italy's Amalfi coast.

The 'Choose Silk' campaign generated a healthy return on investment (ROI), and set Galaxy a clear direction for the future.

LOOKING BACK TO LOOK FORWARD

Galaxy has long been one of the UK's favourite chocolate brands, made famous by its distinctive silky-smooth taste, and its rich history of iconic advertising. The Galaxy girls who featured in the ads were the embodiment of the brand: elegant, stylish and timeless (Figure 1).

Figure 1. Former Galaxy girl

Figure 2. Lounging with Galaxy

However, recently the brand had strayed far from its advertising heritage and had lost the associations that had made it great.

There was little evidence of those compelling Galaxy women who had symbolised the brand so well. Instead, the brand was associated with girls in slippers and pyjamas lounging on the sofa (Figure 2).

What's more, as well as feeling out-of-date, the advertising was becoming less effective year-on-year at promoting brand values and, crucially, at driving sales. To steer the brand back on course, the brand owners needed to understand the background to the problem.

STEERING THE BRAND BACK ON COURSE

Galaxy's recent advertising had resonated in its depiction of chocolate as a pleasure, and sometimes a guilty one, that women wanted to keep all to themselves. The problem with this was that it did not reflect the brand's true values. Gone were the elegance, timelessness and style, and savouring the delicious taste of the chocolate. Instead, it was about chocolate consumption that was both satisfying and secret.

It was essential to make women feel most positive and empowered in choosing Galaxy, like the stars of the advertising in its heyday. So the first step was to undertake scientific research into the taste and eating experience of Galaxy, which found that the Galaxy taste journey is more involving, complex and emotionally resonant than its direct competitors. The finer-milled chocolate produces a sustained sensation in the mouth which lingers longer and delivers a smoother, silkier impression that suggests quality and luxury.

With that compelling product truth the question became: how that could be communicated in a way that truly resonated with consumers? Simply put, how could women be persuaded to choose the better chocolate?

In-depth insights revealed a powerful and universal truth about women Traditionally, the confinement of women's roles in society had made it difficult for them to indulge in time out. Therefore, when women chose to do so, they needed to be confident that it would be worth it, in order to overcome whatever societal expectations might stand in their way.

The communications needed to focus on what made Galaxy chocolate worth overcoming conventions for. And that would be the smooth, silky and lingering taste, which made Galaxy chocolate truly a pleasure worth taking.

So there was now a clear product truth and a rich strategic insight. But that had to be translated into the kind of iconic, powerful advertising that Galaxy deserved. Helpfully, the return of the brand to its positioning as a more refined, sophisticated pleasure would not be unfamiliar to a UK audience. Indeed, the historic endline: 'Why have cotton when you can have silk?' was the perfect encapsulation of the new strategic thought.

WELCOMING THE NEW GALAXY GIRL

It was crucial to find the right type of person to embody this sense of sophistication, while also channelling the confident and inspiring Galaxy girls of the past. She had to represent the duality of the Galaxy personality by showcasing effortless elegance with playful ingenuity. The gamine actress Audrey Hepburn seemed the perfect choice. She was the quintessential Galaxy girl, personifying everything the brand should stand for (Figure 3).

With the Galaxy girl in place and the historic end line resurrected, the next step was to craft a simple narrative of female confidence, daring and ingenuity which emphasised that Galaxy chocolate was a pleasure worth overcoming obstacles for. A significant budget was invested into making a beautiful, show-stopping film which used cutting-edge technology to bring Audrey Hepburn to life.

The Mars team worked with director Danny Kleinman at Rattling Stick, together with Framestore, to make 'Audrey' as true to her image personality as possible, which led to setting the story in the 1950s on the stunning Amalfi coast (Figure 4).

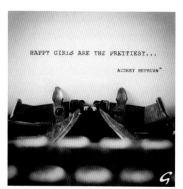

Figure 3. The perfect choice

Figure 4. The perfect setting

Such an exciting and colourful story demanded a media plan to match. It was launched with a bang during the commercial break of *Mr Selfridge*, with the 60-second ad showcased during the first week across the most popular TV shows. Overall, 245 equivalent television viewer ratings (TVRs) were achieved by the end of the week, reaching 68% of all adults.

The TV ad was accompanied by print, digital and out-of-home (OOH) using shots by renowned photographer Mary McCartney, which also featured in national papers, as well as female-focused women's weekly magazines. Overall, a media investment of £7.2 million achieved a reach of 95%, making it truly unmissable (Figures 5, 6 and 7).

To generate excitement and buzz, lifestyle and chocolate bloggers were engaged, as well as key lifestyle media titles such as *Stylist*, *You Magazine* and the *Daily Mail*. They were invited to a special launch event at the Ritz, revealing the new Galaxy girl and premiering the finished film. In addition, the two million-strong Facebook fans were given a preview of the ad with a competition for winners to attend the internal launch party.

Figure 5. Social media campaign

Figure 6. Social media campaign

For that internal launch it seemed entirely fitting to honour the queen of cinema with an outdoor drive-in screening of one of Audrey's classic films in the heart of London. Key celebrity influencers were invited to enjoy the evening, and specifically women who shared the Galaxy girl attitude, such as Daisy Lowe, Emilia Fox and Denise Van Outen. The campaign was accompanied by sampling 600,000 products during the launch period, getting the British public to experience the superior taste of Galaxy chocolate for themselves.

RETURN TO THE GLORY DAYS
In the first three months of the campaign the combined TV ad, print and digital activity delivered a return on investment (ROI) of £1.25 (Source: Kantar World Panel).

Figure 7. Making an impact

The accompanying Facebook element alone generated an ROI of £4.70, with total digital activity returning £2.10, suggesting successful campaign integration across all touchpoints.

There was significant interest in the campaign from trade partners and media, with over 50 pieces of media coverage generating 49,008,000 opportunities to see, resulting in a ROI for the public relations element of £7. The brand also featured in *Marketing* magazine's top 10 most-liked ads of 2013.

Crucially, 2013 ended with Mars block chocolate regaining its number two position in the block category.

CHAPTER 4

04

Mobilising the organisation

Really great and successful organisations realise that marketing can be the driving force for growth in their business.

What Burton's Biscuits, PwC and AMVBBDO have all realised is that great marketing doesn't come by chance. It comes from investing in marketing as a core and vital capability.

For Burton's Biscuits, its investment in marketing capability served to unite the organisation and create an inspiring new vision. The results were exceptional and a clear shift from a function serving the business to one taking the lead.

For PwC, an investment in internal marketing to change pre-conceived ideas and established culture reaped big rewards. The impacts of this campaign are real and long-lasting, and continue to serve as a key differentiator in the highly competitive consultancy space.

Another very different but equally powerful example of mobilising the organisation comes from the AMVBBDO case study. The conception and launch of AMV Bud and the powerful and uniting impact this had on the agency is testament again to the strength of exceptional marketing to positively shift perceptions and drive engagement.

What unites all three is the power of great marketing, uniting and mobilising the organisation for change – marketing excellence in action once again.

Pete Markey
Chief Marketing Officer
Post Office

BURTON'S BISCUIT COMPANY

Enjoying the rewards of a full marketing makeover

SNAPSHOT

A determination to transform the marketing capabilities of Burton's Biscuit Company injected new vigour into brand performance and greatly increased staff satisfaction.

CONSULTANCY

Texo Consulting

KEY INSIGHTS

- A new marketing team set about engineering a revolution in marketing at Burton's Biscuit Company through a carefully-crafted marketing capabilities framework to inject new business growth.
- The resulting programme used a successful combination of workshops, half-day accelerated sessions and a consistent, pragmatic focus on current business issues to embed the new marketing philosophy throughout the company.
- The result has been market share growth, improved brand consideration and a leap in employee engagement.

SUMMARY

Burton's Biscuit Company includes brands such as Cadbury Biscuits, Maryland Cookies, Jammie Dodgers and Wagon Wheels (Cadbury Biscuits are baked in the UK by Burton's Biscuit Company under license). A change of ownership in 2009 resulted in a significant injection of new energy into the business and a revolution in marketing.

Led by the new chief marketing officer and his team, the scale of the task was enormous. The marketing department needed to shift from a function 'supporting' the business to 'leading' the agenda for growing the business through driving sustainable profits from its power brands, developing a healthy innovation pipeline and managing increased brand marketing investment.

A new marketing manifesto was created, using the analogy of 'lighting beacons to show the way' and 'setting fires to drive change' to achieve the company's purpose of 'making every day more of a treat' for consumers, shoppers and employees. To translate the words into action the Burton's Marketing Academy was launched in 2011 to give the marketers the capabilities needed to make this vision a success.

This included the development of a marketing capability framework, workshops, best-practice case studies from within and outside the business, and the embedding of 'hothouse' coaching to ensure all the new tools, processes and templates were applied to all key marketing activities.

It was a two-year programme of change for marketing that reached all parts of the business and transformed the reputation of the marketing team in particular and the business as a whole. Cadbury Biscuits, Maryland, Jammie Dodgers and Wagon Wheels all grew market share, adding value through price and increasing brand consideration scores. Significantly, in November 2013 the company was bought by leading investor and Canadian pension fund Ontario Teachers' Pension Plan for around £350 million, which represented a rise in shareholder value of £200 million since 2009.

Figure 1. Key Burton's brands

GEARING UP FOR A MARKETING REVOLUTION

Burton's Biscuit Company is a leading biscuit manufacturer in the UK, with a portfolio of brands much loved by the British public, such as Cadbury Biscuits, Maryland Cookies, Jammie Dodgers and Wagon Wheels (Figure 1). The company has had many different corporate and financial owners over the past 79 years. However, a change of ownership in 2009 saw a significant step change in the business.

The 'old' Burton's (named Burton's Foods) had delivered little innovation with inconsistent and low levels of brand expenditure and a lack of investment in organisational capabilities. However, with a new owner in place, a mainly-new leadership team appointed and a rebranding of the company to Burton's Biscuit Company, a turnaround plan was developed which focused on power brand growth, a pipeline of new innovation and a significant investment in brand marketing.

To deliver this would require the marketing function to redefine and re-establish itself within the business coupled with a programme to recruit, retain and equip its employees to create and deliver the new business strategy.

In 2010 Stuart Wilson was appointed as the new chief marketing officer and quickly established a 'marketing leadership team'. This was a group of individuals who had built their marketing careers in well-known consumer goods companies such as Mars, Kraft, Kellogg's, InBev, Nestlé and Kerry Foods but were all looking for a new challenge.

The first objective was to set out the purpose of the marketing department in this 'new' business. It was no longer to be about the marketing department 'supporting' the business but leading it to drive sustainable profit growth through its power brands. The ethos of 'lighting beacons to show the way' and 'setting fires to drive change' was at the heart of the marketing manifesto.

The key strategies were centred on:
• Insights to deliver outstanding innovation to market.
• Exciting consumers and shoppers to choose the brands again and again through brilliant innovation, distinctive communications, superior product quality, pitch-perfect packaging, smarter promotions and revenue management.
• Constantly beating the competition by focusing on driving value market share growth, ensuring that the share of innovation is twice market share and securing sources of sustainable competitive advantage.
• Executing with excellence to build legacies that last a lifetime.

Underpinning these were some challenging objectives set for the marketing team:
• **Leadership** through outstanding collaborative working and excellent project delivery.
• **Superior commercial understanding** of the competitive environment and business.
• **Accountability** for the resources they manage and the investment they make.

- **Development** of a highly-motivated team of talented individuals.
- **Enjoyment and pride** in their achievements, learning from mistakes and celebrating successes.

ESTABLISHING THE RIGHT FRAMEWORK

The marketing team knew from the start that the approach taken had to mirror the culture of the business and help marketers meet the requirements of the new manifesto. They had to be pragmatic and nimble and make sure everything was tailored to the very fast-paced nature of the work that Burton's marketers do every day.

So they began by defining a capability framework based on the marketing manifesto set out by the chief marketing officer and his leadership team. It was practical, easy to use and showed the entire team what was expected of them across all key competencies in order for them to achieve their aims and continue making future progress (Figure 2).

Key Marketing Competencies at Burton's

Figure 2. Key marketing competencies   Figure 3. Marketing Academy workshop programme

The leadership team then rated the current capabilities of the marketing function to determine the areas of development where they could create the biggest impact on the business as quickly as possible. The capability framework also set out very clearly the key content areas for the Burton's Marketing Academy workshops (Figure 3).

At this point it was also agreed that the Marketing Academy would consist of both functional and leadership capability-building since leading the business in marketing thinking was seen as such a critical competence in order to fulfil the new manifesto.

The team continued with the theme of 'pragmatism' in establishing the Academy workshops. The workshops were highly-interactive two-day offsite sessions focusing on 'big win' skill sets to support marketers in line with the marketing capability framework. With each workshop 'owned' by a member of the leadership team, the content evolved continuously to reinforce the key marketing tools and processes that needed to be embedded.

The Burton's team, along with Texo Consulting, ensured that the workshops included those templates, tools or processes which were the most relevant, up-to-date and, most importantly, tailored precisely to Burton's needs.

KEEPING IT REAL

All the exercises the delegates undertook in the workshops were based on real marketing issues at the company. The overarching purpose was straightforward: delegates should walk out of the workshops having developed something they needed to do anyway but also having learned along the way – and done it better than they could have done back in the office. This could include a brand plan, a 'killer' insight, brand positioning or an innovative idea (Figure 4). Constant feedback was collected so that the content stayed relevant.

Figure 4. Workshops in action

Workshops were scheduled around the business planning cycle to ensure timely inputs to marketing thinking. Where relevant, invitations were extended to other functions to promote joined-up thinking and shared visions. There were inputs of best practice and case studies from agency partners and, without fail, each member of the marketing leadership team, including the chief marketing officer, attended every workshop to coach, facilitate the learnings and inspire the participants. Feedback was excellent and workshops were scored consistently with ratings of 4.8 out of 5, with particularly high scores for 'I am able to apply this to my role immediately'.

In addition to the workshops for all the team members, 'hothouses' were developed to provide every brand team with a bespoke, follow-up facilitated session for a half-day to embed the tools and processes from the Academy and apply them to a current brand opportunity or issue.

Again, the focus was on keeping the programme pragmatic and relevant. Marketers had to be working on something that they already needed to deliver to the business with the aim of improving it in a consistent way. With groups of no more than six people, these 'hothouses' produced excellent results.

RESHAPING THE BUSINESS

The results have transformed the company's marketing abilities and ultimately business performance through the impact of sharper insights, outstanding innovation that consumers genuinely want, breakthrough communication strategies and bringing brands to life through excellent project delivery.

All of this has been reflected in the performance of the power brands (Figure 5). Moreover, the company's brand success has been acclaimed through a number of key awards (along with the winning award for this case study):
- *Grocer* Gold NPD of the Year 2011
- Tesco NPD of the Year 2011
- *Asian Trader* NPD of the Year 2011
- Marketing Society Awards for Excellence 2011
- 2013 IGD Industry Award for Consumer and Shopper Excellence
- 2013 *Grocer* Award for 'Top Launch of the Year' in the biscuits category and 'Top Campaign' for the Maryland Gooeys TV campaign

Strong 'Power Brand' growth in market share and improved brand consideration

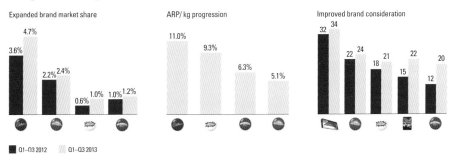

Figure 5. Strong power brand growth

Source: Drelsen, Millward Brown

Furthermore, the company completes an annual engagement survey across the whole business, encompassing over 30 engagement metrics. Over the past three years the overall marketing engagement score has grown, while, significantly, the metric for 'I feel well-trained to do my job' (Figure 6) has increased and clearly been driven by the Marketing Academy programme. The programme has also led to a number of well-deserved internal promotions among the company's marketing team.

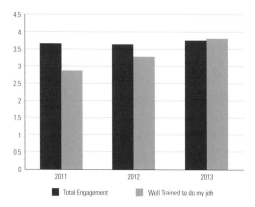

Figure 6. Increase in employee engagement

KEY LEARNINGS FROM THE BURTON'S MARKETING CAPABILITY PROGRAMME

- Think hard about the culture of the business you are in and match the capability development approach to the culture for the best chance of success.
- Being pragmatic and flexible is essential in developing a capability programme. Focus on 'quick big wins' and the rest will follow.
- Marketing development programmes can play an important role in improving current performance as well as for global business development and/or for an individual's long-term career enhancement.
- Always work with something relevant to the business in workshops to make a measurable difference to the delivery of existing projects.

All images appearing in this case study are reproduced by permission of Burton's Biscuit Company.

PwC
Pioneering a radical shift in ways of working

SNAPSHOT

In a determined bid to cut down on the impact of travel on carbon emissions PwC set in place a witty and persuasive integrated campaign which convinced staff of the benefits of meeting online.

AGENCY

Civilian

KEY INSIGHTS

- The professional services firm was keen to drive through a programme to cut down on high levels of business travel and hence its carbon footprint.
- A clever, multi-channel campaign used the story of a relationship developing through online meetings to increase both awareness and ultimately usage of online meeting technology.
- Not only were carbon emissions cut significantly, but the positive return on investment showed that benefitting the business and the environment were not mutually exclusive.

SUMMARY

PwC is one of the world's largest professional services networks. As with most professional services firms, its business is built on relationships and trust, which by its very nature demands the personal touch: meeting face to face, shaking hands, making eye contact. But PwC was aware that being there in person means travel, and travel had come to make up more than half of its carbon footprint.

So, in March 2012, it launched a campaign with a grand ambition: to challenge long-established ways of working. The firm wanted to enable its people to make different choices about when to travel and when to stay put. That called for making much greater use of travel alternatives such as web and video conferencing.

A campaign was developed that told the story of two people whose relationship blossomed through the use of online meetings. But was the relationship professional or personal? The ambiguity was never quite resolved. That sense of intrigue, as well as the innovative use of new channels and an integrated campaign across every one of its 30 UK offices, produced results that speak for themselves.

From a negligible base, the campaign achieved 30% penetration, a 409% increase in usage, and a lasting shift in perceptions. At the same time, the carbon footprint dropped 7.4% while, significantly, revenues increased, thus helping to decouple the environmental impacts from business growth. In addition, the campaign delivered a pronounced return on investment (ROI), saving an estimated £37 in travel costs for every £1 spent.

SETTING AMBITIOUS OBJECTIVES
PwC's product is unquestionably its people. Getting them in front of clients is an essential part of winning and doing work. Consequently, carbon emissions from travel constitutes a large part of its overall footprint: 55% in the year to June 2012. That included travel of almost 135 million miles, at a cost to the business of £45.2 million. That's why, despite the firm's determined ambition to grow the business over the next five years, it has committed itself to keeping emissions from travel at their 2007 levels.

Obviously, travel can't be avoided entirely. But the firm believes that, in some circumstances, web and video conferencing offer a viable alternative to travel, allowing its people to work just as effectively while lowering costs, improving well-being and reducing the environmental impact.

Admittedly, as a services business, PwC's environmental impacts are low in comparison to many sectors. But its sustainability strategy commits it to 'doing the right thing' and to acting as a 'catalyst for change'. Tough targets have been set: to reduce, by 2017, all material and waste impacts by 50% and total carbon emissions (including travel) by 25%.

The need to decouple environmental impacts from economic growth is a fundamental principle underpinning efforts to limit the impact of climate change. Sustainable consumption has a key part to play in this.

So the firm decided to capitalise on the roll-out of a new online meetings system, WebEx, to promote new ways of working. It wanted its people to feel comfortable connecting remotely and using collaborative technologies to work with one another from anywhere in the world. In turn, the travel and carbon footprint would decrease. The overall aim was to reduce the carbon footprint of its services and make the 'consumption' of them by its clients more sustainable.

That called for three key objectives:

1. Change perceptions of alternatives to travel. In March 2012, just over a third of PwC's people felt that online meetings were appropriate for working on a client engagement. Most saw web and video conferencing as difficult, risky and unreliable. To boost take-up, the team in charge of the campaign would have to change these perceptions fundamentally.

2. Drive use of online meetings. In the 12 months before the campaign, the firm's 17,400 people organised just 6,027 online meetings. An awareness campaign would simply not be enough. People needed to be encouraged to trial the technology and have a positive experience, so there was a base from which to build frequency.

3. Help to decouple economic and environmental impacts. Between July 2009 and June 2012, a 10% growth in revenues contributed to a 23% growth in carbon emissions from business travel. WebEx usage had to translate into fewer journeys to help achieve the wider aim of breaking the historic correlation between the environmental effects of business and growth.

Figure 1a,b,c. The campaign concept

COMPELLING COMMUNICATIONS

Working with Civilian, a marketing agency specialising in sustainable behaviours, the PwC team developed a campaign concept which centred on a blossoming relationship and a strong, action-oriented strapline – "Make a date with WebEx" – to promote the new, preferred online meetings tool (Figure 1a,b,c).

The campaign was designed to be upbeat and positive in tone, and used clever, witty copy that would appeal to the workforce and link online meetings to the clear business benefit of building strong relationships.

Because the aim was culture change across such a large organisation, the campaign needed longevity. So the concept allowed for multiple phases to keep the messaging alive and fresh, and showcase different aspects of the technology's functionality. All the waves included a clear call to action to drive trial of the new system.

The team set out three strategic principles to help meet the objectives:
1. Get people's attention in a crowded communications environment.
2. Convince them of the benefits of WebEx so they'd want to try it out for themselves.
3. Finally, make it as easy as possible for them to get started and to feel comfortable with the technology.

1. Get noticed

To achieve high impact, the campaign was launched across multiple channels in every one of the firm's 30 UK offices on the same day – something that had never previously happened before. To stand out from the crowd, it made creative use of simple, bold colours and typeface, while remaining true to the PwC brand. The heart shape, which made the materials instantly recognisable, was attached to collateral including posters (Figure 2) and table talkers with adhesive to give a greater sense of depth and texture.

Figure 2. Poster

Figure 3. Microsite

A strong physical presence in the offices was matched across digital channels, including the kiosks that people used to book a desk in the morning, the network of office plasma screens, emails and a dedicated microsite (Figure 3). The main campaign was complemented and achieved greater cut-through with a teaser promotion: heart-shaped 'stickies' in a bright pink envelope were sent to everyone via their personal pigeon holes (Figure 4). The stickies just announced the beginning of 'the story', accompanied by the opening 'We just clicked' strapline, creating buzz and intrigue.

To maximise the impact and associate sustainability with innovation, some new in-office channels were developed which included working with the firm's vending

Figure 4. Teaser promotion

Figure 5. Vending machine

machine providers to create new poster points where there was a guaranteed captive audience (Figure 5). And, in meeting rooms across all of the 30 offices, tailored flip chart covers were used to talk to the target audience about alternatives to travel in a context in which these messages would intuitively make sense to them.

2. Sell the benefits
The team in charge of the project knew that many of the firm's people were sceptical about the reliability of video and web conferencing and considered these tools to be complex to set up and run. The campaign messaging systematically set out to challenge and reverse these perceptions.

3. Make it easy
Awareness alone wasn't going to be enough, however, so a set of resources was developed to make it as easy as possible for people to trial the software, including:
- A series of short, online demos, accessed from the campaign microsite.
- Weekly, online, drop-in 'surgeries' which were called 'WebEx Wednesdays'.
- A dedicated section of the firm's social media platform, Spark.
- Downloadable user guides (Figure 6).

Figure 6. User guide

CHANGING MINDS
The campaign delivered a fundamental shift in perceptions among the firm's people, helping to unblock a deep-rooted scepticism, create positive associations and double the number of people who felt that WebEx has a role to play in working with each other and with clients. For instance:
- In March 2012 36% of those surveyed felt online meetings were appropriate for use when working on a client engagement. Confidence in video conferencing and online meeting tools was also low.
- By January 2014, 79% felt online meetings were appropriate for use when working on a client engagement. 78% of meeting organisers said they felt confident using WebEx, while 80% said WebEx was easy to use.

Numbers of online meetings hosted by UK staff every quarter rose dramatically by 409%, from just under 1,500 before the campaign to almost 7,500 at the end of 2013. Periods of significant growth in WebEx use have followed campaign activity. To put this in perspective, it would have taken 15 years to reach this level had growth continued at its pre-campaign rate.

In April 2013, PwC began to measure the proportion of its people who were taking part in WebEx meetings each quarter. Over the subsequent nine months, penetration almost doubled, from 18% to 30% (5,249 people). This increase was important because it was indicative of widespread adoption of this new, more sustainable way of working (Figure 7).

PwC measures and reports on its carbon footprint at the end of each financial year. The years prior to the campaign highlighted what seemed to be an inexorable link between travel and revenues. In fact, travel emissions had been growing disproportionately. The results published in 2013 showed a reversal in this trend: the year-on-year revenues continued to rise, but the carbon footprint dropped by 7.4% (Figure 8).

MAKING A BIG DIFFERENCE

Return on investment was also very positive: the money invested in the campaign delivered measureable benefits, both to the business and more widely.

In January 2014, PwC surveyed 250 WebEx users about the extent to which they used online meetings to avoid travel. The results enabled the firm to estimate the savings generated from online meeting use over the previous 12 months. Over the course of the campaign, people ran 34,937 online meetings (with a total attendance of 189,972).

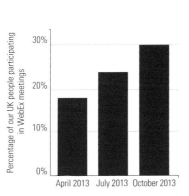

Figure 7. Online meetings increase

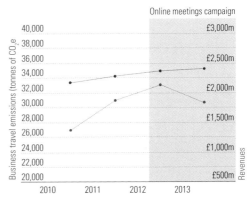

Figure 8. Carbon emission drop

Of these, it is estimated that 19,700 sessions could be attributed to the campaign. Survey results suggested that this equated to around 8,700 return journeys avoided (excluding commuting). This would have cost more than £4.1 million had people travelled instead. This implies a saving equivalent to around £37 for every £1 spent on the marketing campaign.

LONGER-TERM BENEFITS

A key tenet of sustainability is 'externalities': impacts which are not covered by existing financial accounting methodologies. Over the past few years, and separately from the sustainable behaviours described above, PwC has been working with others to put a monetary value on these impacts and pioneer new forms of measurement. The 'social cost of carbon' is a measurement of the current and future costs of incremental damage caused by climate change, resulting from the emission of an additional tonne of CO_2 today. In 2013, the social cost of carbon was estimated to be £52/tonne CO_2. On this basis, the campaign saved an additional, estimated £127,700 in abated carbon emissions.

All images appearing in this case study are reproduced by permission of PwC.

AMVBBDO
Giving staff a renewed sense of service

SNAPSHOT

The communications agency was determined to boost employee motivation and hence client satisfaction through a company-wide event that would get all staff to appreciate its strong charitable ethos.

KEY INSIGHTS

- Despite attracting numerous accolades for its working environment AMVBBDO's leaders felt there was a gap between what it actually did in terms of giving back to society and what its employees perceived it did.
- Highly aware of the proven link between employee satisfaction and business success, the agency used its creative capability to devise an ambitious charitable fund-raising programme to involve every single member of staff.
- Not only did it comfortably hit its target for fundraising, but the longer-term impact on employee motivation is already showing through in terms of business performance.

SUMMARY

AMV, founded in 1979 by David Abbott, Peter Mead and Adrian Vickers, is the biggest communications agency in the UK in terms of revenues. It is part of the BBDO network, the third largest agency network in the world. AMVBBDO has produced an array of award-winning campaigns for some of the UK's and the world's leading brands. In 2012 it was ranked as the best advertising agency and the 17th best company generally to work for in the country by *The Sunday Times*.

The agency has always been heavily involved in charity work, including acting as patron for the London-based charity Kids Company. However, its leaders felt there was a gap between what the agency did and what its people perceived it did. Its solution was to embark on a major company-wide event spearheaded by the development of a new brand, AMV Bud, to represent how the agency could make a difference to the world.

An event was created to bring the brand to life. It was a six-day relay from John O'Groats to its London offices with a format to give anyone who wanted a chance to take part. Along with producing great team spirit, it raised £32,000 for the chosen charity, Brain Tumour Research. It also achieved its overall objective of seeing a pronounced rise in employee satisfaction which, in turn, has had a measurable impact on client satisfaction.

CLOSING THE GAP

Throughout its 35-year history, AMV had prided itself on its strong focus on employee satisfaction, appreciating the proven link between motivated employees and customer loyalty and profitability. Consistently high scores of client satisfaction had been the result.

In addition, the agency had been demonstrably active in charity work over the years. For example, it was a patron of a London-based charity called Kids Company while its group chairman was on the fundraising board of Comic Relief and its CEO the chairman of the National Advertising Benevolent Society.

However, the agency was well aware that, operating in one of the most intensely competitive markets in the world, it couldn't afford to be complacent and needed to keep innovating to stay ahead. Further investigation found that there was room for improvement in what it actually did in terms of its charitable work and employee perception of how the agency 'gave back' to society.

So attention was turned to the cause of this gap. Reviewing its legacy, the agency's leadership team asked itself whether enough had been done in recent years to inspire and motivate staff to appreciate that the company they worked for really did seek to make a difference.

That led to the realisation that more needed to be done to ensure that the firm commitment to charitable endeavours was appreciated by every single member of staff. Added incentive to tackle this came from an understanding of the service-profit chain, a management theory which has demonstrated the connections between employee satisfaction, improved client relationships and business and profit growth.

It decided to tackle the issue with the same resolve it applied to clients' problems. So the first step was to design a brand – AMV Bud – to symbolise the new initiative (Figure 1). Employees were asked to nominate and vote on which charity Bud should raise money for to give them all a stake in the campaign. The winner was Brain Tumour Research, a charity that had supported a colleague during his illness.

Figure 1. Bud Logo

This was followed by the creation of an ambitious and challenging agency-wide event: a 25-leg multi-disciplinary relay from John O'Groats to AMV's offices in London, taking place over six days in September and dubbed AMVBBDGo (Figure 2). The relay format meant that something different could be done for each leg, playing to people's special talents and preferences. There would also be a final leg that would involve every single person in the agency.

Figure 2. The route

GETTING IT TOGETHER

Engaging the employees before the kick-off was critical to its success. The event was launched by the CEO at the bi-monthly all-agency meeting using a promotional video, as well as posters that went up around the agency. The appeal went out for 25 team leaders who would effectively act as the brand influencers, recruiting people and getting them excited at ground level.

The team leaders were given a distance they had to cover and a time they had to complete the leg in. How they did this was up to them, whether it be cycling, running, walking, swimming, skateboarding, dancing, a pram push, or trolley dash or even pedi-bus.

People were encouraged to set up their own 'Just Giving' pages on the BBDGo site while teams were urged to organise their own fundraisers every Friday in the run-up to the event. The fundraisers included cake sales, a race night, a cinema trip, a BBDGo burger being sold at a local pub, the services of a copywriter (who offered to write to any brief), and the ubiquitous charity box. Staff were also asked to choose what fancy (silly) dress the senior executives including the CEO, head of project management and the board planner should wear on their hitchhike leg.

Once the relay was opened up to entrants, more than 212 people applied with over 200 agreeing to take part in the final leg. Finally, a sponsor video was produced that employees could send out to friends and family to encourage donations.

MAKING THEIR MARK

Excitement mounted as the relay went live, with employees posting regular updates and messages of support. There were nearly 400 tweets about the event reaching more than 50,000 people.

Each leg was tracked with GPS-connected devices so the participants knew exactly how many miles they had done and how far they had to go (Figure 3).

Momentum built throughout the week as the first relay participants returned home to tell of their triumphs and new fresh-legged participants nervously left to embark on their own challenges. By the third day, it had really taken off. And for the 'finale' on day six, everyone got involved by walking from Hyde Park back to AMV for the final baton handover (Figures 4 and 5).

Figure 3. Tracking the journey

Figure 4. Bringing the baton home

Figure 5. The final handover

In the end, 412 people covered 842 miles in 25 different ways over just six days. These efforts raised an impressive £32,000, which put the agency in the top 5% in terms of donations in 2013 (Figure 6). Employee satisfaction also increased considerably, with a far higher proportion agreeing that the organisation had made a positive difference to the world they live in.

Significantly, it also correlated with business growth in the months directly after the event, with the agency winning substantial new business from blue-chip clients such as Dixons Retail and Guinness.

Figure 6. Badge of honour

CHAPTER 5

Building powerful new brands

Marketing convention tells us that launching new brands is a risky business. The cost of start-up and the risk of failure are high, a recipe for losing a lot of money. It is therefore incredibly stimulating to read these four case studies of successful new brand launches.

So what is it that each of these stories has in common? I think the secret is that all are based upon a simple insight and provide a new product or service which is truly distinctive.

Hailo followed a succession of very similar apps but was the first to put the cab driver first and really understand the issue of isolation that they experience. It was therefore the first cab-hailing app that really worked for cab drivers and as a result the most successful of all.

McLaren and Jack Daniel's took the time to deeply understand their core brand values and successfully enter highly competitive markets with distinctive new brands.

BT Sport was probably the most bold of all, taking on the might of Sky with two high quality sports channels that were free to BT broadband customers. The insight couldn't have been clearer (we all love free stuff) but the audacity is admirable and the quality of both the product and the launch communications to be admired.

So while convention might tell you that creating new brands is not for the faint-hearted, these four stories tell us that a combination of clear insight, a distinctive offering and unwavering boldness can reap huge rewards.

Jon Goldstone
Vice-President, Brand Building,
Foods and Ice Cream
Unilever UK & Ireland

MCLAREN
From super car to brand superstar

SNAPSHOT

McLaren took the courageous decision to extend its winning position beyond Formula 1 and build a brand for the road.

AGENCY

VCCP London

KEY INSIGHTS

- McLaren's triumphs on the racing track brought it much sporting and technological success but little success as a brand in its own right.
- Its determination to find success on the road as well as the track in the face of well-entrenched Italian icons demanded not just building a brand but developing a new business model encompassing production, distribution and marketing.
- In just 18 months the brand captured a quarter of market share against the key models of the two biggest competitors.

SUMMARY

McLaren had long had a sterling reputation for sporting success, having accumulated a series of trophies from the Formula 1 racing arena. So when the company decided to move into road cars with a business model that would demand strong branding, production scale, a quite different target audience and new distribution channel, it faced a formidable task.

Even more dauntingly, the company would be taking on those Italian stars of the highways, Lamborghini and Ferrari. To do this, it had to prove it could overcome some big challenges: that it was a manufacturer and retailer, rather than a race team only, and that as a brand it could hold its own in glossy showrooms as well as on Grand Prix race tracks. Working with VCCP London, McLaren's approach revolved around one core marketing strategy: 'Fuel the myth'. This would emphasise stories about McLaren's colourful heritage rather than its state-of-the-art technology. It would need to be reflected across all areas of the marketing mix, from uniforms through to motor shows.

The first dealership opened at a prestigious central London address. In just 18 months, the brand captured more than a quarter share against the two biggest competitors.

BOLD BID TO BUILD A BRAND

Ferrari and Lamborghini are two of the most recognisable and desirable brands on the planet (Figure 1).
- Ferrari was created by racing enthusiast Enzo Ferrari. In 1929 he started selling cars to fund his racing. His brand was valued in Interbrand's *Best Global Brands* 2012 at $3.7 billion.
- Lamborghini was established in 1963 by Ferruccio Lamborghini, who set out to establish a glamorous touring car.

Purchase of the heart
Wow   Looks
Proud   Beauty
Ferrari Community
     Fantasy Style
Emotional   TR
Alredo Ferrari Iconic
Italian Enzo Ferrari
    Passion Visually
History   Respect

Super car
Luxury car
Italian   German
Power   Looks
Sounds
        Heaven
Prestigious

Figure 1. Desirable brands

While they are distinct brands, they share striking similarities. Their appeal is universal and transcends race, religion or class. Both are obviously Italian and are seen to have extravagant and passionate theatrical personalities full of flare. Attitude is as important to these brands as engineering. They appeal to hearts and heads almost equally.

By comparison, McLaren heralded from much more humble beginnings. New Zealander Bruce McLaren started his race team in 1963 in a garage in Woking, competing in the Canadian-American Challenge Cup, or Can-Am. And, while the team might have lacked Italian flamboyance, it more than made up for it in racing performance, dominating the original Can-Am series with 43 wins. That success led to Grand Prix racing, where McLaren began to come up against the more 'fashionable' side of motor sport.

While the rivalry between McLaren and Ferrari had always been fierce on the track, as brands they were almost diametrically opposed. In fact, McLaren couldn't really be called a brand. The prancing horse of Ferrari and the 'rossa corsa' or racing red of Italian teams had been liberally deployed in a variety of ways, from ultra-exclusive vehicles like the FXX (which costs $1.8 million and can only be driven on certain days on certain tracks) down to mass-produced key chains, not to mention the famous Ferrari World theme parks.

1963-1966	1967-1980	1981-1990

1997-1997	1997-2002	2002-2012

Figure 2. McLaren brand over time

By comparison, the British-run McLaren was a shifting amalgamation of the brands which sponsored it. That's because it was primarily a racing team and a media owner. In its entire 50-year history its owners had never seen the value in developing its own brand (Figure 2). The business model instead combined technical excellence with business savvy: McLaren was paid to build sponsors' brands, not its own.

The aim was simple but very ambitious: to create a sports car brand to rival the main models of Ferrari and Lamborghini, the Ferrari 458 and the Lamborghini Gallardo, and quickly establish a foothold in the market. But this would be much easier said than done. The list of failed supercar brands was almost as long as the list of failed Formula 1 teams. Examples such as British brand TVR's famous roller-coaster ride of success, failure, success and its ultimate demise (TVR was once the third-largest maker of specialised sports cars in the world) demonstrated the difficulty of taking on legacy marques and making them successful.

McLaren thus had some difficult decisions to make in a number of areas:

- **Business model.** McLaren Automotive would have to become a manufacturer and retailer rather than a race team/media owner.
- **Production.** This new strategy would require a steep change in manufacturing capabilities.
- **Place.** Rivalries would no longer be fought on greasy pit lanes and Grand Prix tracks but on the polished floors of plush dealerships.
- **Mindset.** Formula 1 races are won (among other things) by hard-earned technological advantages that can be copied relatively easily. It's no wonder that successful teams are fundamentally and organisationally secretive. But McLaren would need to tell stories to survive.
- **Audience.** While the 'aspirant masses' are vital to sales as they give permission to purchase, the new audience were prospects who probably already had supercars in their garages, not posters on their walls. This was where a real difference could be made to McLaren's road business.

TELLING THE RIGHT STORY

Technical mastery defines McLaren. The McLaren Technology Centre (MTC) is designed entirely for the purpose of creating winning vehicles. It is dedicated to understanding machinery. The shift from track to road, however, required a much deeper understanding of sports car drivers and their motivation. Research was conducted on wealthy prospects, the people who worked with them and the experts who understood them best. Two key audience insights were uncovered.

The first came from a conversation with Elizabeth Sieff, founding partner of Little Emperors, a concierge service to the rich and famous: "It's not about fashion anymore. That's boring. It's everything related to technology: Apple, tablets, home entertainment and the environment. That's what's turning people on right now."

This sentiment helped free the brand from any lingering desire to challenge the Italian brands on fashion because it emphasised that the tide was turning against the shallow, fashionista brands as the luxury world searched for more substance. It would benefit the McLaren brand to continue to be driven by aesthetics and style but to avoid anything as fickle as 'fashion'. The new heroes should be revolutionary thinkers like Steve Jobs of Apple and Google's Sergey Brin.

The second audience insight came courtesy of a broker for Burgess Yachts. Jonathan Beckett helped the brand's owner to understand fully the power in successful luxury brands, in that it doesn't really come from the products sold but from the stories they possess: "They've already got the biggest and the best. It's the story that makes something truly valuable."

The McLaren product was definitely world-beating, born from the hard-won experience of a Formula 1 patriarch. The Italians might have their pouting pit girls and flaming exhausts, but McLaren had something a bit deeper: iconic names like Bruce McLaren, Ayrton Senna, Lewis Hamilton and Jenson Button. This wasn't about ostentatious luxury but was about a Formula 1 legend for the road.

So the strategy would revolve around one core marketing message: "Fuel the myth". This wasn't a challenge that would be met by advertising alone. All elements of the marketing mix would be needed, from the uniforms to the floor tiles to the motor shows. The big difference with the competitor brands was embedded in McLaren's values: innovation, courage and obsession. A successful strategy had to be based on all those working together.

Racing was the source of the two most important ingredients (Figure 3):
• **Rational:** expertise and technology informing the road car from that of the track.
• **Emotional:** deep heritage infusing the brand mythology.

The audience wanted to buy into a myth. But to tell it straight was the quickest way to shatter it. Advertising was essential, but it wasn't going to meet the brand's challenge alone. It would be critical to find the right brand ambassadors who would be empowered to tell its story.

Figure 3. Brand heritage

LAP TIMES

1. Pagani Huayra   1.13.8
2. Ariel Atom V8 500   1.15.1
3. McLaren MP4-12C   1.16.2
4. Bugatti Veyron Supersport   1.16.8
5. Gumpert Apollo   1.17.1
6. Lamborghini Aventador   1.17.1
7. Ascari A10   1.17.3
8. Koenigsegg CCX (with Top Gear spoiler)   1.17.6
9. Pagani Zonda F Roadster   1.17.8
10. Nissan GT-R (2012)   1.17.8
11. Caterham R500   1.17.9
12. Bugati Veyron   1.18.3
13. Pagani Zonda F   1.18.4
14. Maserati MC12   1.18.9
15. Ferrari Enzo   1.19.0
16. Porsche 911 GT2 (997)   1.19.5 (pd)
17. Ariel Atom   1.19.5
18. Lamborghini LP560   1.19.5 (pd)
19. Porsche 911 GT2   1.19.5 (pd)
20. Ferrari Scuderia   1.19.7
21. Nissan GT-R   1.19.7
22. Porsche Carrera GT   1.19.8
23. Lamborghini LP640   1.19.8
24. Koenigsegg CCX   1.20.4
25. Ascari KZ1   1.20.7

"It is one of the fastest road cars in the world right now."

Figure 4. Top Gear leader board

The one thing McLaren had going for it without any doubt was technical ability. The machine was going to do the talking for that expertise. And it did, with the brand coming third in the TV programme *Top Gear's* leader board (Figure 4). It placed it behind the Ariel Atom and the Pagani, which costs roughly four times as much. It also beat the Bugatti Veyron, the £1.5 million hyper-car *de jour* and the world's fastest production car (assuming there were no corners, of course).

All this would mean nothing if the marque didn't answer the audience's basic questions since, generally speaking, these weren't people who would spend £200,000 without doing their homework. The car would have to be priced cleverly and widely available to compete with the Ferrari and Lamborghini.

A BRAND STAR IS BORN
Product
The product was without doubt outstanding. Born in the same building as the track car, it was not only inspired by its development but included technology that was actually banned in Formula 1. BrakeSteer, a system that applies braking to the inside rear wheel during cornering to pivot the car around a corner, was developed by the team in 1997 but banned for giving an unfair advantage on the track. It was a key selling proposition and enhanced the sense of myth and history of the physical product.

In fact, as Figure 5 shows, the product out-performed the competition in all the important numbers.

	Ferrari 458 Italia	Lamborghini Gallardo	McLaren MP4-12C
Power	570 PS	560 PS	600 PS
Torque	540 Nm	540 Nm	600 Nm
Weight/Power Ratio	2.9 kg/PS	2.9 kg/PS	2.6 kg/PS
0-60 (mph)	3.4s	3.7s	3.1s
Top speed (mph)	202	202	207

Figure 5. Competitor statistics

Pricing

In terms of pricing, McLaren placed itself just under the Ferrari and above the Lamborghini. This was high enough to give the product initial credibility but low enough to force serious consideration by the competitors' loyalists (Figure 6).

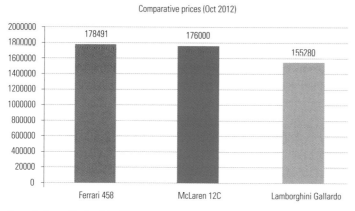

Figure 6. Competitor's pricing (£)

Distribution

Meanwhile, the dealerships gave what had seemed to be a formerly reclusive brand a physical presence. The first flagship store was located in a very prominent London location: 3 Hyde Park. And, within 18 months, McLaren had gone from having no dealerships to having 36 operating in 20 countries. This was an impressive achievement but it was still a small fraction of that of the competition, which had a presence ten

Figure 7. McLaren showroom

times greater than McLaren's. The showrooms exhibited quality, not quantity, bringing the brand's story to life as an emotional, tactile experience. Each contained one of McLaren's historic Formula 1 cars (Figure 7).

While the 12C was the launch car, the next model, the McLaren P1, was revealed towards the end of 2012 at the Paris Motor Show. This was another important opportunity for McLaren to fuel the myth, with Ron Dennis launching the car in front of an orange Formula 1 race car so there could be no mistaking the brand's pedigree (Figure 8).

While the brief wouldn't be fully answered by advertising, the dealership network would need a flexible suite of ads to use in their own markets (Figure 9). This was an ideal way to solidify the message of the new brand, with the campaign balancing the need for elegance required in luxury publications with the grittier link to racing.

Figure 8. Paris Motor Show

Figure 9. Dealership network adverts

Internally, the brand's heroes were being celebrated and a film created to give voice to the legacy of Bruce McLaren. It was released to the public in 2013 to celebrate its 50th birthday.

CROSSING THE FINISHING LINE

Between 2008 and 2010 McLaren sold no sports cars. In 2011, 210 cars were sold. By 2012 that had risen to 1,398 sports cars. Thus, from a standing start and with a tiny fraction of the showroom real estate, McLaren had taken on the established might of the super car market and carved itself a more-than-sizeable foothold. In just 12 months 1,608 cars were sold. Significantly, the brand captured a quarter of the market share against the two biggest competitors for their key models (Figure 10).

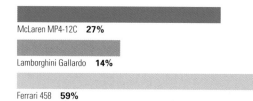

McLaren MP4-12C **27%**

Lamborghini Gallardo **14%**

Ferrari 458 **59%**

Figure 10. Value share against competitors 2012 (Jan to Oct)

All images appearing in this case study are reproduced by permission of McLaren.

JACK DANIEL'S TENNESSEE HONEY

The sweet taste of success

SNAPSHOT

The makers of one of the world's most iconic brands took the spirits market by storm with the launch of the first flavour extension in over ten years.

KEY INSIGHTS

- The owners of the best-selling whiskey in the world, Jack Daniel's, were keen to grab the attention of a new generation without diluting the strong values of the parent brand.
- They launched the new drink, made from whiskey with added honey, with a carefully-staged and comprehensive campaign that embraced both traditional platforms and social media to create buzz.
- The result was the biggest spirits launch in the UK in the past five years.

SUMMARY

Jack Daniel's, part of the Brown-Forman brand portfolio, is a global iconic brand and the best-selling whiskey in the world. However, the company wanted to ensure that the brand continued to resonate with a younger generation who, research said, are more experimental, less loyal and love novelty.

The company was keen to capitalise on the strong brand values of the main whiskey brand of independence, authenticity and integrity while offering younger drinkers a drink more palatable to their tastes. However, the introduction of Tennessee Honey was a big step for Brown-Forman as it was the first flavour extension from the Jack Daniel Distillery. If done incorrectly there was much at stake.

The result was Tennessee Honey, the first new product from the Jack Daniel Distillery in over a decade. Launched in May 2011, its success encouraged the company to enter the UK market a year later. Social media and customer relationship management were used to build excitement among the brand's core fans, while the ensuing through-the-line campaign saw it become the biggest spirit launch in the UK in the last five years.

The line extension added significant incremental volume to current and long term forecasts. Research confirmed minimal cannibalisation and that Tennessee Honey had had a positive "halo" effect on Jack Daniel's Old No 7.

FINDING A WAY TO A YOUNGER AUDIENCE

Jack Daniel's is a brand that has been carefully built behind three core values: authenticity, integrity, and importantly, independence. Strong adherence to these values have helped it grow in strength from generation to generation to the point where it is the best-selling whiskey in the world (Figure 1).

Its credentials are impressive:
- It's a global icon that has become bigger than the whiskey itself.
- It is consistently listed in Interbrand's top 100 global brands.
- It sells over 10 million 9-litre cases worldwide and is the fourth biggest spirit brand.
- It is sold in more than 160 countries, with every drop made in Lynchburg, Tennessee.
- It has won seven gold medals since 1904.

Figure 1. The Jack Daniel's family

However, research had told the company that while the Jack Daniel's brand still resonated with the millennial generation, their behaviours were different from the previous generation. They had more choice in drinks than ever before, while loyalty was less important. They were experimental and always seeking to try new products, while they valued fun and novelty in flavours, colours and formats. They also drank more in mixed-gender groups, which had an obvious influence on what they chose since they catered for the group.

After all, millennials have grown up in an era when most packaged goods, from confectionery to crisps to water offer flavour and variety. Why should their spirit brands be any different? And, while they loved the brand (and the T-shirts), many found the idea of drinking whiskey a bit intimidating and preferred sweeter, more palatable drinks.

The company's solution to this was the first launch of a flavour extension by the Jack Daniel Distillery in over ten years. However, great care and patience was taken until the product was absolutely right because of the potential impact on the parent brand from cannibalisation, among other concerns.

For example, the packaging and liquid needed to align precisely with the Jack Daniel's brand. So the package was designed to feature the familiar, iconic square bottle with a cream label and hints of gold that promise the delicious character of Jack Daniel's Whiskey and real honey flavour (Figure 2). The label communicates the classic brand with a twist that is an invitation to a drinkable, subtly sweet product with a very natural look and feel, in keeping with the image of honey itself. The bee icon is prominently featured as a signal of the honey used in the drink, as well as exemplifying the "swarm" of Jack Daniel's consumers around the world (Figure 3).

The drink itself is crafted by adding honey liqueur to Jack Daniel's Old No 7, creating a taste that is authentically Jack and naturally smooth.

Figure 2. The new brand   Figure 3. The bee icon

LAUNCHING ACROSS CHANNELS IN THE UK

Following a successful US launch in May 2011, the company decided to bring it to the UK a year later. There were two key objectives: introduce a new audience to Jack Daniel's and get existing Jack drinkers excited about a change to the whiskey they love.

Social media and customer relationship management (CRM) were key elements in building excitement and introducing the new variant to the brand's fans first. This was important since the brand had a large and loyal fan base who could be used to help spread the word of the new drink.

The campaign was run on a number of platforms:
- For example, the launch email saw open rates of over 30% and click-through rates over 65%, while there were 34,000 competition entries for the first 100 bottles of Tennessee Honey.
- Twitter and blogging sites were used to spread the message teasers and video to new consumers while the Facebook page also attracted a lot of visitors.
- During this time the brand was seeded in the on-trade, with the launch to the off-trade in August.
- Accompanying that was a major campaign across TV, cinema, digital and outdoor.

The main creative content told a story about a beekeeper, a honey bee, rock 'n roll and whiskey. The first part of the story involved four teaser videos featuring a Jack Daniel's beekeeper making honey (Figure 4). This was followed by an animated ad featuring a honey bee with Jack Daniel's in its DNA in a 30" TV spot with a rock 'n roll soundtrack. The campaign message of "A little bit of Honey. A whole lot of Jack" was visualised through a playful king bee 'ripping' through a bottle of Jack to reveal Tennessee Honey.

Figure 4. The beekeeper

Exploiting the digital platform to reach these millennials was essential. So the playful king bee was sent to rip through key desktop and mobile websites to reveal Tennessee Honey. The company also devised a bespoke campaign for Spotify and Xbox to get the brand into occasions where consumers would get together with friends at home.

TV and cinema were used to drive mass awareness but in a competitive environment the brand needed to stand out. Because cinema is such a key media for this audience, the company created a cinema ad to get them talking to their friends about the brand. To give it 'buzz', it began with 10 seconds of black screen and the sounds of swarming bees. In 2013 that was followed by a king bee 3D ad to coincide with the high-profile release of *Star Trek Into Darkness*.

Other imaginative media included a British taxi (Figure 5) and posters on London Underground – a popular medium for the parent brand – and the Glasgow Subway (Figure 6). Trialling also played a significant role: the company knew that the more the drink was sampled, the more it would benefit from word-of-mouth.

Figure 5. London taxi

Figure 6. Glasgow Underground poster

BREAKING NEW RECORDS

The success of Tennessee Honey far exceeded the company's expectations. It has added incremental volume to the spirits category with very little cannibalisation (Figure 7). Other results underline the effect of its launch:

- It soon equated to more than 10% of Jack Daniel's Old No7 in the UK while having a 'halo' effect on Jack Daniel's itself, which saw growth of 4.5% moving annual total (MAT) volume in the UK in 2013.
- It was the biggest new spirit launch in the US in 2011 and the biggest spirit launch in the UK in the last five years.
- Within a year of its launch, when compared to sales of products in the imported whiskey category, Tennessee Honey was in third place behind Jack Daniel's and Jameson and had out-sold the whole Jim Beam range combined.

Adding incremental volume to the spirits category with minimal cannibalisation

Jack Daniel's Honey – Shifting gains & losses (total spirits)
– Total Coverage – 36 weeks to 27.04.13 vs. YA

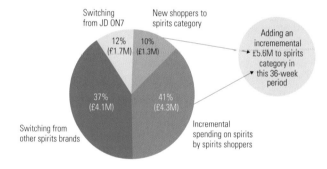

Figure 7. Adding category volume

Imported whiskey is now the second fastest-growing category in spirits. Significantly, the brand extension is bringing in a new generation of drinkers to the Jack Daniel's brand while attracting existing Jack drinkers as well, adding substantial incremental volume and profit to the UK and global business.

BT SPORT
Rewriting the rules of brand building

SNAPSHOT

BT shook up the broadcast market with its audacious launch of two new premium sports channels offered free to current customers in a bid to revitalise its brand performance.

AGENCY

AMVBBDO

KEY INSIGHTS

- BT was determined to gain a more dominant position in the market for broadband customers who were increasingly keen to bundle TV, broadband and phone services in one package.
- Aware that premium TV content was key to winning business from rivals like Sky, BT stunned the market with the launch of two new sports channels with proprietary content.
- But the real shock was its decision to offer the channels to customers for free, a decision which ultimately rewarded it both in terms of brand perception and business results.

SUMMARY

BT is one of the world's leading communications services companies. It operates in more than 170 countries worldwide and offers fixed-line services, broadband, mobile and TV products and services as well as networked IT services. In the UK the former state telecoms provider sells products and services to consumers, small- and medium-sized enterprises and the public sector.

For consumers, that includes BT-branded fixed-line, broadband and TV services directly to UK homes. The market is intensely competitive, with at least a dozen bundled product suppliers and over 100 fixed-line operators. The four largest suppliers are BT, Sky, Virgin Media and TalkTalk.

In 2012, despite its prominent position, research had shown that the public's perception of BT was that of a slightly old-fashioned company with a heritage in cables, whereas Sky was viewed as more contemporary and modern, resulting in a particularly loyal customer base. Sky was thus stealing a march within the broadband acquisitions market since more customers wanted to bundle their phone, broadband and TV services into one convenient package.

To strengthen its brand positioning compared to its rivals BT decided to do something dramatic. In 2013 it launched BT Sport 1 and 2 with proprietary, premium sports content broadcast from a state-of-the-art studio. However, in a move that really grabbed the market's attention, the company announced that it would be giving BT Sport to its customer broadband base for free.

Despite dire warnings from some commentators that this would be disastrous for the business, the bold move paid off handsomely. Not only did a number of brand affinity measures rise significantly after the launch, but the company saw a substantial return on its investment.

Preparing to do battle

In 2012 the four main brands battling it out for supremacy in the telecommunications market were (and still are) Sky, Virgin, BT and TalkTalk. In this sector, it is generally accepted that the best way to win customer favour within the category is to provide a really good TV service. People are loyal to brands that provide popular programmes, are prepared to pay a premium for those brands and despite that price premium believe those brands to provide better overall value for money.

At the time, Sky was rated as providing the best TV service, with its customer advocacy, satisfaction, value for money and customer effort scores well above those of BT, which languished in third place. BT was seen as a slightly old-fashioned company with a heritage in cable, whereas Sky was contemporary and modern because of its association with TV.

The big problem for BT was that the customer dynamic within the phone/broadband/ TV market was towards what's called the 'triple play', or customers bundling all three services into one supplier. People were proving to be particularly loyal to Sky because of its TV service, so they were choosing their broadband and phone services to go with their TV package. So Sky was stealing a march within the broadband acquisitions market.

BT, on the other hand, was seen as first and foremost a broadband company. This was unsurprising: it owned the pipes in the ground and made money by selling them to consumers. To confront the challenge of Sky using the power and magnetism of its TV service to steal share of the broadband market demanded something dramatic.

SHAKING UP THE MARKET

The company knew that if proprietary content was the way to stem the flow of broadband churn to Sky, then it had to be premium content that the nation would want to watch. And that meant premium sports content.

So, in a move that took the market aback, BT bid and won the rights to broadcast 25% of the 2013/14 Barclay's Premier League televised games, including half of the 'Top Pick' games (Figures 1 and 2), all of the Aviva Rugby Premierships (Figure 3), various other football leagues from around the world, the Women's Association of Tennis

Figure 1. Premier League football

Figure 2. Premier League football

Figure 3. Rugby

Figure 4. ATP Tours

Professionals (ATP) Tennis Tour (Figure 4) and all of Moto GP, the premier motorcycle racing world championship, with the promise of even more to follow.

This content would be shown on two new premium live sports channels (BT Sport 1 and 2 in both standard and high definition) and served by a brand-new, state-of-the-art studio at the Olympic Park. BT lured top talent such as anchorman Jake Humphrey (Figure 5) plus experts and pundits like Michael Owen, Lawrence Dallaglio, Austen Healey and Claire Balding to front the broadcasts. To get this off the ground would also call for a heavyweight, through-the-line communications campaign.

This was a bold and audacious strike at Sky's position. Since 1992 when Sky had helped transform the old First Division into the Premiership, it had become synonymous with almost all televised sport in the UK, and especially football. It would place huge demands on BT: billions rather than millions of pounds in terms of investment. The enormity of the initiative and the subsequent risk to the overall business should the venture fail to pay back could not be underestimated.

As one City newspaper put it at the time, the high-risk strategy was looking like a 'very expensive kamikaze mission'. But even that was trumped by BT's next announcement: it would be giving BT Sport to its entire broadband customer base – then around 4.5 million UK households – for free. In other words, the company was giving away the service for free but still determined to get a good return on its investment.

CONNECTING THE DOTS

BT's strategy was finely judged. People liked and were loyal to Sky because of the great TV and particularly the sport. BT, on the other hand, was seen as an old-fashioned, pipes-in-the-ground company that was invisible when things were going right but moaned about when they weren't. So selling sport in the same way as Sky would have limited results for a number of reasons:

• The amount of sport/content BT had in relation to Sky was still very small, so the amount of favour to be gained was much lower.
• There were a group of diehard fans who had to have access to every televised game. They would have bought BT Sport on top of their Sky Sports package but

Figure 5. Jake Humphrey

would most likely have resented BT for having to pay twice.

- There was another set of customers who liked sport but didn't have Sky Sports because it was too expensive. They might have bought BT Sport if they thought it looked good enough (i.e. much better than the forerunners of BT as an alternative to Sky, such as Setanta and ESPN) and was significantly less expensive. BT would thus have ended up with a core audience of customers expecting a lot for not very much.
- There were also millions of UK households who liked sport but would never pay for it because they believed they shouldn't have to. To them BT Sport would be just another brand, charging for something they believed they should be able to access for free.

However, if BT offered the sports content for free to its entire broadband customer base these potential drawbacks would no longer apply:

- It wouldn't matter that BT Sport was smaller than Sky Sports because it was free.
- Diehard Sky Sports fans could still get all their sport at no extra cost.
- An entire generation of sport-loving households who didn't want to pay for sport could now watch it thanks to BT.

That all seemed very promising, but the pivotal issue was the potential impact on BT's business performance. However, the company was convinced its plans were sound:

- Giving BT Sport free to existing BT Broadband customers would make them feel valued and rewarded and reduce churn.
- It would give new BT Broadband customers a reason to choose BT over other broadband providers that didn't offer free sport (all of them) and would drive customer acquisition.
- Giving BT Sport for free to BT Broadband customers provided an opportunity to charge non-BT Broadband customers (£12 a month) which, in turn, created a new revenue stream for the business that was beyond the existing customer base (subscription-only customers).
- The channel would also generate more advertising revenue because it was free, as the viewing figures would be higher.

When looked at in this way, it seemed clear that giving BT Sport away for free actually increased its value to the business compared to selling it direct to consumers as a subscription model. What at first looked paradoxical in fact made very good business sense.

REAPING THE REWARDS

BT's bold move paid off handsomely. First, in terms of 'net brand advocacy' BT closed the gap with Sky Sports by a substantial 17% thanks to the new service. Given that the total amount of content BT provided was still relatively small, it could be assumed that the 'free' aspect contributed hugely to the growth in more positive brand advocacy scores (Figure 6).

Net Advocacy Score – BT's Gap to Sky

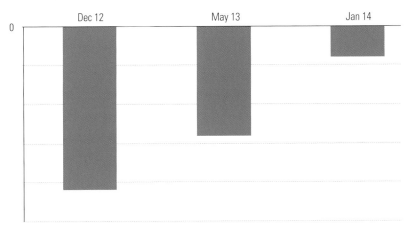

Figure 6. Net advocacy score: gap decreases   Source: GfK BT Consumer Tracker Questionnaire 2014

Brand 'warmth' metrics also increased significantly in areas such as 'BT keeps me better connected to the people and things I love', 'BT makes products that keep me entertained' and 'BT helps me get more out of my relationships'.

Crucially, business performance also benefitted in three substantial ways:
• The lifetime value of customer acquisitions and retentions created by BT Sport.
• The lifetime value of BT Broadband customers who paid for a subscription to the channel.
• The advertising revenue generated by BT Sport.

The positive performance of those three measures meant that, as a comparison, if the returns against the initial investment were to be indexed at 100, the return on investment (ROI) was £4.80 for every £1 spent. The launch also saw the BT's share value enjoy a 44% rise.

All images appearing in this case study are reproduced by permission of BT.

HAILO
Breathing new life into an old market

SNAPSHOT
A new branded app created to connect taxi drivers with passengers transformed the fading fortunes of London black cab drivers.

AGENCY
Rothco

KEY INSIGHTS
- Hailo's founders were convinced that an app to connect London taxi drivers and passengers would revolutionise what had been a relatively inefficient market while creating a network to end driver isolation.
- The fact that three of the founders had been taxi drivers meant that the business model reflected the realities faced by both drivers and consumers.
- By the end of 2013 a Londoner was getting into a Hailo taxi every six seconds.

SUMMARY
Hailo is a free smartphone app which puts people just two taps away from a licensed vehicle and enables drivers to get more passengers when they want them. A Hailo hail is now accepted around the world every two seconds from Hailo's global network of over 50,000 drivers and more than a million passengers. However, looking back to the London taxi market before Hailo launched in November 2011, the landscape was grim. Drivers were faced with 30% to 60% downtime affecting their bottom line. The business model of street hailing was under threat as impatient consumers found it increasingly easy and desirable to order in advance.

Hailo was determined to remedy this with an app that connected drivers and passengers. The fact that the company's founders included three taxi drivers ensured that the company was well-placed to differentiate itself in the market. Integral to the point of difference was that the app focused not just on passengers but on the drivers as well by connecting them to each other.

By November 2013, Hailo had become London's number one taxi app, with a Londoner getting into a Hailo taxi every 6 seconds. The company had surpassed four million journeys and become the highest rated taxi app on the iTunes and Android stores.

TAXING TIMES

Hailing a taxi in London was becoming less common, with the black cab market under threat and facing a year on year decline. On a daily basis, drivers were facing a harsh reality with 30% to 60% downtime affecting their bottom line. The business model of street hailing was under threat.

Impatient, time-pressed commuters were turning to other options that better suited their lifestyles, organising cabs in advance rather than taking a gamble in attempting to hail one on the street. Private hire firms such as Addison Lee and local mini-cab companies were capitalising on the changing needs of passengers, and began to lure passengers away from black cabs at an alarming rate.

By August 2011, Addison Lee had reported profit growth up by 62% to £7.6 million for the year. Company reports also showed the group's turnover rose by one-fifth to £127.5 million during the same period. The rise in licensed private hire vehicles and drivers was significant (Figure 1).

Licensed private hire vehicles and drivers in London

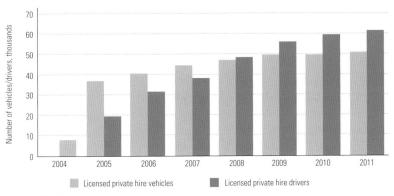

Figure 1. Significant market growth

Leading up to 2011, eight companies had spotted the inefficiency in the black cab market and produced apps that allowed Londoners to hail a black cab from their smartphones. Apps like GetTaxi, Kerb, Taxi App and BlackCabNow were gaining traction with the concept of the 'mobile hail'. With a primarily passenger focus, they put control into the hands of the public who could demand a cab at the touch of a button.

By 2011, according to the *Economist*, six of the taxi apps had fallen by the wayside, with only one remaining. This differed from the other apps in that it placed a greater importance on drivers by kitting out the taxis with GPS systems at no cost, and by looking after the maintenance of the drivers' data plans.

BUILDING A NEW MODEL

In December 2010 three technology entrepreneurs spotted the inefficiencies in the market and decided to build a cab app with a difference. Their background in corporate logistics quickly helped them realise how the cab experience could be made better. Contrary to the other cab apps that focused on the passengers' user experience, they believed that in order to make the best product and overall experience, they needed to focus on the drivers.

Armed with this belief, the entrepreneurs met with three former London black cab drivers who had fifty years experience between them. By the end of their initial meeting, Hailo was conceived, and the six founders were in agreement that the app should be built upon driver experience insight.

The three driver founders shared the insight, issues and needs experienced by black cab drivers. They brainstormed the key issues with the three entrepreneur founders, and collectively identified that the biggest problem facing drivers was isolation. Drivers experienced isolation in two distinct ways, both of which seriously impacted their business.

1. Isolation from potential passengers (and thereby income)
Drivers make up just one half of the cab. Passengers account for the other half. But potential passengers no longer saw black cabs as always being the most convenient option. Modern commuters have high expectations and are less prepared to wait around. Technology and constant access to information has led them to 'on demand' services that allow them to remain in control without breaking their stride (eg mobile banking, shopping, Sky+ and online check-in).

As everyday modern life speeds up, there are more demands placed on our time, with more little things to have to stop and worry about. New technologies are thus embraced not just because they are new, but also because they allow us to have control. This in turn simplifies life. Things run more smoothly, conveniently and faster, with less hassle and distraction. The more time spent doing what one wants to do without being slowed down, distracted or 'paused' by unnecessary things, the better.

2. Isolation from other drivers

A black cab driver's job is by its very nature an 'isolated' job. They work on their own, in their own cabs and have to take responsibility for themselves. They cannot rely on anybody else. There was no way to predict or plan the day ahead, and drivers would often rely on luck to navigate through whatever London presented in search of a fare.

Drivers also struggled harder to find fares because potential passengers were turning to options other than the street hail. Drivers thus craved connection to both demand from customers and the support that a network could provide.

In response to this double-edged sword, Hailo built itself upon two strategic ideas that truly connected the black cab driver:

1. Connecting drivers and passengers.

Hailo instantly connected empty cabs to the people who wanted one. With just two taps, a black cab was within arm's reach of commuters. It also provided a further convenience for drivers and passengers by making it possible to pay by credit card, eliminating the hassle of having to stop at an ATM or drivers having to refuse a fare.

2. Building the driver community

To remedy driver isolation, the founders felt it was paramount to supply, as part of the foundation of the product, a framework through which drivers could connect with one another. The Real Time Events feed available in the driver's version of the app functioned as a social media platform: it was a news feed which allowed drivers to update their status, providing other cabbies with important information such as where more cabs were needed and which streets to avoid due to traffic. As well as making it easier for drivers to find more jobs, avoid traffic, etc., it crucially helped them keep in touch with other drivers.

GEARING UP FOR LAUNCH

With product development well underway, Hailo needed to prepare a launch to both drivers and passengers that would create instant demand and pull. With relatively modest budgets, a clear and powerful brand idea that conveyed the purpose, benefit, and reason for existence of the brand was essential.

The Hailo marketing team worked closely with Rothco to develop a brand book that was based on the original brand identity work done by Daren Cook Associates, but would also reflect the company's overall values i.e. that Hailo always strives to make things easier for both drivers and passengers by removing pain points – as well as the feel and tone of voice of the brand.

The epitome of the brand book was a simple, driver – and passenger – unifying brand idea: the Taxi Magnet (Figure 2).

Figure 2. Taxi Magnet

The benefits to the drivers included:
• Removing isolation.
• Connections to other drivers.
• Connections to passengers.

For passengers, the benefits were:
• More control.
• Connections to taxis.

The immediate task of the launch communications strategy was to drive understanding, awareness and therefore trial of the app. Two principles of engagement informed the approach:
• The audience was drivers as well as passengers.
• Drivers would be key in recruiting other drivers as well as busy and elusive passengers.

That meant that the communications had to follow a multi-layered approach.

1. Drivers first
Drivers were the first target. Because there could be no better advocates for black cabs than black cabs themselves, drivers were empowered to play a vital role in winning back their work.

Two driver-empowering initiatives were implemented at launch:
• Livery Programme. Hailo drivers were incentivised to adopt exterior and/or interior branding to gain on-street presence, and the perception of a fleet (Figure 3).
• Cabbie Code Programme. Through in-cab driver promotion and signage, unique 'Cabbie Codes' enabled passengers to redeem £5 credit towards their first card account journey for which drivers received a £2 bonus. Cabbie Codes gave cabbies an easy conversation starter to promote Hailo, drive trial, and generate word-of-mouth publicity.

Figure 3. Full livery

2. Public relations (PR) and outreach
Understanding the importance of recommendations from trusted sources, brand ambassadors were identified and engaged at launch.
• Ambassador engagement kicked off during the Chelsea Flower Show. Former Chelsea gold medal-winning designer Ian Drummond transformed three Hailo cabs into gardens, transporting people to and from the flower show in an initiative that afforded Hailo great coverage in numerous publications.
• Key influencers in fashion, music and food were offered free trials of Hailo. Mentions from the likes of Lorraine Pascale, Giles Coren, Tim Westwood, Lisa Snowdon,

Lauren Laverne, Chase & Status, Fashion Foie Gras, Henry Holland, *Stylist* magazine and Tali Lennox meant Londoners had millions of opportunities to see.
• Profile slots were secured for several of the founders: Jay Bregman, Russell Hall, Ron Zeghibe and Caspar Woolley.
• Acclaimed photographer and blogger Victoria Hannan showcased the driver community.

The creative approach kept the brand's profile high. For example:
• The founders and investors made announcements to attract mass coverage and were profiled in business publications/sections with heavy taxi-user reach.
• Sir Richard Branson publicised (in a photo call and interview) the news that over half of the black cab drivers in London had signed up to Hailo, garnering coverage in the *Evening Standard, Huffington Post*, the *Telegraph*, the *Independent*, Bloomberg and City A.M., among others (Figure 4).
• Showcasing Hailo drivers' legendary London street knowledge by identifying outdated road signs and creating new signage, which generated mass coverage and sparked conversations, featuring prominently in the *Times, Daily Mail*, Yahoo, *Huffington Post*, and on LBC.

Figure 4. Sir Richard Branson

3. The communications plan

The communications plan was developed to support and boost awareness of the trial-driving campaign, targeting both drivers and passengers. For drivers, 'Back in Black' championed the black cab industry and imbued a sense of pride in their legendary role in London. Using visual cues from the app, the work communicated that even though you might not see a black cab right in front of you, you could now connect with those in the vicinity.

For passengers, it was a call to action to get back into black cabs, supported with the end line: 'Black cabs just got easier'.

The media was specifically selected to target commuters in areas of high footfall. The two-week campaign consisted of:
- Outdoor: back-lit signs and billboards at major train stations, posters on major high streets and digital billboards in Canary Wharf and along the A13 into London.
- Press material focused on London's free commuter newspapers, as well as magazines (i.e. *Time Out*).
- Online consisted of Facebook App Install ads, display and social media promotion such as competitions to share photos of how you got back in black and win Hailo credits.

4. Partnerships

The success of the awareness campaigns allowed the business the freedom to focus on market expansion from the mid-to-end of the second year. More passengers were hailing cabs through the app, and now it was time to encourage them to use it from home. And the Hailo from Home campaign aimed to take Hailo further afield as well.

Through partnerships with Ocado, Hello Fresh, Taste of London and the *Evening Standard*, £5 vouchers for Hailo were put into the hands of passengers in their homes, making the appeal of Hailo even stronger since it was just a touch of a button away from your sofa. As well as partnership vouchering, which reached millions of people, other initiatives across London reinforced the Hailo From Home message:
- Door-dropped leaflets offering residents a voucher on their first booking (Figure 5).
- Branded phone boxes across London.
- Hailo cab interiors transformed to look like living rooms.

Figure 5. Door-drop leaflet

WINNING THE BATTLE

By November 2013 Hailo had become London's number one taxi app. A Londoner was getting into a Hailo cab every six seconds, with over four million journeys and an app that had become the highest-rated taxi app on iTunes and Android stores.

In addition, over half of all black cab drivers in London had registered with Hailo, delivering each driver an average of three jobs per day in addition to street hails, while passengers also embraced the app.

Hailo was presented with prestigious awards in the UK in 2013:
• Tech City Future Fifty Programme (selected by the UK government)
• *Sunday Times* Tech Track, winner 'Ones to Watch'
• The Next Web UK Start Up of the Year
• Appster Awards: Most Innovative App and Best Payment Solution

All images appearing in this case study are reproduced by permission of Hailo.

CHAPTER 6
Building global brands

06

Being in over 74 markets and a true international bank, building a global brand has always been a critical part of our strategy. With perpetual technological advances, coupled with the increasing use of digital platforms, the world is becoming a smaller place, allowing brands to cross international borders with growing ease. Reading these case studies helps to highlight the core principles that provide the foundations of building a successful global brand.

1) Build a strong and consistent brand culture from the inside out, that remains familiar to customers wherever they are in the world. Unilever's Axe brand is tightly targeted at young men as they make the transition from boyhood to manhood. The 'angel' concept was relevant to young men wherever they were in the world and kept to the brand's key message of 'seduction'.

2) Borderless marketing. The Famous Grouse built a global integrated marketing campaign that was based on its famous icon's quirky personality and used the device wherever it ran.

3) Build an internal central hub. The communication ideas in Axe were created centrally. It was vital that each of the 100 markets adopted the campaign to deliver a consistent brand voice and identity across the globe.

4) Create a 'glocal' structure. The Famous Grouse brand mounted its biggest ever global campaign 'Famous for a reason', using through-the-line tools that could easily be adapted at a local level in markets such as Russia and Greece.

5) Use consumers as co-creators.
Global qualitative research produced a sharp universal insight that the actual fantasy of an 'Axe guy' was a 'nice girl'; not the 'naughty girls' young men were presumed to be after!

Amanda Rendle
Global Head of Marketing,
Commercial Banking and
Global Banking and Markets
HSBC

THE FAMOUS GROUSE

Celebrating 30 years of global brand building

SNAPSHOT

The Famous Grouse marked its position as Scotland's best-selling whisky with a high-profile global campaign that spanned countries and cultures.

AGENCY

The BIG Partnership

KEY INSIGHTS

- Edrington was determined to use the 30th birthday of its leading whisky brand to increase sales and grow the brand.
- It built a multi-channel, integrated global campaign that was based on its famous icon's quirky personality but which was flexible enough to be tailored for quite different markets.
- Its 'Famous for a reason' message translated into a sales uplift of more than 8%.

SUMMARY

Edrington, owner of The Famous Grouse brand, wanted to celebrate its 30 years as Scotland's best-selling whisky. It decided to mount the brand's biggest-ever global campaign, 'Famous for a reason', which was based on an integrated, multi-channel strategy built to offer a set of through-the-line tools that could easily be adapted at a local level in markets such as Russia and Greece. Techniques included advertising, PR, on-trade activity, digital, point-of-sale and packaging.

It began on 4 May 2010 with an event at the distillery in Scotland for 1,200 guests from around the world. One-metre high grouse icons were on show before being given as gifts to key markets, where they were decorated by artists from each country to attract local publicity.

Overall, 23 markets representing 85% of sales adopted the campaign and were able to adapt it according to local needs. In mature markets such as the UK 'Famous for a reason' provided fresh impetus for the brand. An online campaign launched on Facebook sought nominations for the best bars which provided a good boost to the on-trade. The top 30 pubs were enlisted into the Grouse Trail with an illustration created for each one.

The campaign reached more than 24 million consumers, increasing sales significantly and resulting in substantial brand growth.

EMBARKING ON A MOMENTOUS JOURNEY

The Famous Grouse first attained its status as the number one selling whisky in Scotland in 1980 (even though it costs more, the Scots choose it over any other Scotch whisky), a position it has held onto ever since (Figure 1). And so, in 2010, The Famous Grouse chose to mark this very happy birthday with a series of events and promotions across the Scotch whisky-sipping globe.

The Famous Grouse wanted to say a big 'thank you' to those who had first put and then kept the brand at the top of the tree. And for those who had still not made The Famous Grouse a central part of their whisky-sampling world, this was a chance to let them know what they were missing. Above all, consumers and traders needed to know that The Famous Grouse is 'Famous for a reason'.

Figure 1. The Famous Grouse

The strategy was to create a 360° through-the-line campaign with its PR agency, that could easily be adopted in all markets. The campaign included: advertising, press trips, and events; fresh packaging and special edition bottles; trade campaigns such as voting for bars which were 'Famous for a reason' and The Grouse Trail featuring designed replica grouse.

The overall aim was to increase the reach among current consumers and to entice the light buyer. Promotional and marketing activity would revolve around the 'Famous for a reason' message and The Grouse Trail, integrating on-trade, digital and PR activity. It would be the widest-reaching global campaign in the company's history, comprising 23 significant market campaigns, representing 85% of global volume and reaching upwards of 24 million consumers.

The objectives were ambitious:
- Clearly convey the No.1 whisky in Scotland message in the warm and witty 'Grouse' tone of voice.
- Communicate the 'Famous for a reason' message.
- Increase reach and saliency among current consumers and reassure light buyers by giving them a reason to believe in the brand.
- To provide every market with a clear 360° campaign that would enable them to develop and deliver these objectives easily.

BLAZING A TRAIL

Because August 12th marked the brand's birthday, it was considered the ideal date to launch the campaign. The 100-day countdown began on 4th May, alerting consumers and markets to the forthcoming celebrations. To kick things off, an open day was held at the distillery and, with over 1,200 visitors, it was the busiest day ever (Figure 2). A special Birthday Trusadh (the name of the company's brand education programme) took place at the distillery, with invitations for journalists and VIPs from Russia, Portugal, Sweden, Greece and India.

The most ambitious part of the campaign was The Grouse Trail. The Famous Grouse stands apart from its competitors because it is named not after the whisky's founder, but after Scotland's national game bird – the red grouse. The Grouse Trail involved celebrating the icon by creating replicas of 'the grouse', each measuring one metre high. After an initial celebration at the home of the brand, the models then embarked on a world tour which would see them decorated by artists from different countries. This gave each market free reign to choose a local artist and create a bespoke PR story.

Figure 2. Open day at distillery

Figure 3. Grouse statue

To make this truly memorable, the company decided to set itself the challenge of creating a grouse statue at the home of the brand in Perth. As a result, a permanent statue was erected in Perth, towering above the A9 at the Broxden roundabout, which is one of the busiest roundabouts in Scotland. The sculpture, which depicts a grouse taking flight, can be seen emerging from the trees on the roundabout. Standing proud at an impressive 49 ft tall (including the 29 ft column) and weighing 1.5 tonnes, the sculpture promises to be one of the most striking public artworks in Scotland (Figure 3).

This open structure of galvanised steel was created by Scottish sculptor Ruaraig Maciver. Favourable comparisons have been made to the famous Angel of the North near Newcastle. By working tirelessly with the local council and Transport Scotland, the company was given permission to create the eye-catching sculpture to celebrate Perth 800.

Perth 800 was a year-long celebration in 2010 which marked the 800th anniversary of the granting of the Royal Burgh Charter to Perth by King William the Lion in 1210. It was agreed that the red grouse is a fitting symbol of Perthshire and so the sculpture was gifted to the people of Perth.

ALL AROUND THE WORLD

Over 22 markets, accounting for over 80% of The Famous Grouse sales, adopted the campaign, making it the single most successful campaign the company has rolled out to date. Three markets have been chosen for this case study to illustrate how they each conveyed the message that The Famous Grouse is proud to have spent 30 years at the top of the whisky league.

RUSSIA

The team in Russia enthusiastically embraced all different aspects of the campaign.

- The website www.famous30.ru was the main hub of activity, with competitions and games for consumers to play.
- Facebook was used to reach the core target audience of trendsetting 30-year-olds and attracted over 3,000 members. The Facebook account featured reports from events and links to promotional activities on the website, helping to create a strong buzz.
- With the slogan 'Let's celebrate together' ringing loud and clear, The Famous Bar promotion allied to www.famous30.ru was launched to help choose the best bars in Moscow and St. Petersburg. Bloggers, photographers and bagpipers were recruited to get the celebrations started.
- Bottle neck-hangers were placed in all stores, inviting people to visit the website.
- Limited edition 30-year-old blended malt and Timorous Beasties gift tins were developed to provide another PR news-hook.
- Famous Dinners were held for VIPs and media-generating press coverage appeared in glossies such as *Playboy*, *Medved*, and *My Way*, while press trips to Scotland resulted in double-page spreads published in a range of high profile magazines, including *Transaero-Imperial* and *Menu*.
- The Famous Grouse also sponsored a range of events, including tastings and a concert by iconic Scots rockers Nazareth, as well as 'Famous' dinners in Volgograd and Rostov.

Hitting the right note with consumers
- Brand tracking showed that the PR activity had a high level of cut-through, with around a quarter (26%) of people interviewed claiming to have seen articles about The Famous Grouse.
- Visitor numbers to the campaign website following the launch almost doubled.
- The campaign reached over 10,000 consumers on Facebook, with an average of 3,150 comments, which demonstrated the extent of audience engagement.

UK AND GREECE

Both the UK and Greece chose to celebrate 'Famous for a reason' with campaigns that integrated advertising, on-trade, digital and PR activity. In what were tough, mature markets, the campaigns enabled the teams to encourage brand engagement by giving consumers and the on-trade the reasons why The Famous Grouse was worth paying more for.

- Famous 100 pubs and The Grouse Trail in the UK were an opportunity to thank the on-trade for their support in making The Famous Grouse, Scotland's No.1 selling whisky for 30 years. As a result of its success it was rolled out for a second year and won four industry awards.
- Famous 75 Bars and The Grouse Trail in Greece offered opportunities to reach key influencers as well as directly engage the 30-year-old target audience through Facebook and targeting the on-trade.

1. UK: The Famous 100 Pubs

To celebrate the long-lasting success of the brand and bring to life the 'Famous for a reason' message, the UK launched a campaign to find 100 famous British pubs (Figures 4 and 5). As the British public have a strong emotional relationship with their local pubs, and most pubs have a famous story, they asked people to nominate why their local should be made famous. The best 100 would be celebrated in a bespoke 16-page supplement in a national newspaper, *The Daily Telegraph*.

Figure 4. Famous 100 Pubs campaign   Figure 5. Famous 100 Pubs campaign

There were a number of objectives:
- Bring to life the 'Famous for a reason' message for both consumer and trade.
- Drive traffic to the microsite and secure a minimum of 400 nominations.
- Get coverage throughout the country about the nominated pubs and their reason for being famous.
- Switch drinkers to The Famous Grouse from other blended whisky brands, retain these consumers and build emotional engagement via the 'Famous for a reason' message.

The campaign was a striking example of an integrated campaign that engaged both the on-trade and consumer audiences to generate coverage for the brand. It achieved:
- 43,000 hits.
- 11,000 unique users.
- 800 online nominations (double the target set).
- Along with publicity from having a national media partner, the nominations also provided rich material to create significant regional and online coverage, with 53 pieces appearing across the seven regions.

The quality of the nominations submitted was exceptional. As a result, The Famous 100 became a fantastic collection of renowned pubs that truly stood-out from the crowd. The 16-page supplement included inns, pubs and hotels of all shapes and sizes. Their reasons for being famous ranged from a pub in a cave, another with a boxing ring, to one that leans further than the leaning tower of Pisa (see 'Feedback from publicans').

The results showed that the objectives were met and exceeded:
- It brought the slogan 'Famous for a reason' to life for consumers while supporting key outlets.
- The brand could capitalise on the genuine fame it enjoyed from 'Famous for a reason'.
- Buy-in by the trade and semi-permanent/permanent branding provided strong switching messages at point-of-purchase.
- The on-trade outlets received 'free' publicity as a result of being in the Famous 100.
- This will grow each year as more pubs are inducted to The Famous Grouse 'Hall of Fame' annually.

FEEDBACK FROM PUBLICANS

Leila Maia (Barley Mow pub)

"We are so proud to be in the 'Famous Top 100'. The timing of the award was fantastic as we had just had a refurbishment so our guests had seen the amount of work that went into it. They have also been talking about it and bringing the supplement in to show us."

Stuart Wraith (Fools Nook)

"The Famous Grouse Famous 100 is a wonderful idea, celebrating the interesting histories of these typically British institutions. Not only highlighting our heritage but finding out about others was fantastic."

The Grouse Trail
The UK Grouse Trail was launched in April 2011 via Facebook to identify the 30 favourite pubs from The Famous 100. The Famous Grouse then recruited Scottish artist Johanna Basford to create an illustration representing each of the favourite 30 pubs. These were drawn onto the Grouse replica, which then toured the UK.

The campaign peaked with the release of the 30 designs for each of the famous pubs (Figure 6). To maximise exposure, two-dimensional versions of the designs were shared individually via Facebook and Twitter, generating a lot of excitement and comments from fans. Regionalised press releases were issued announcing the 30 pubs across the UK that would receive a bespoke Johanna Basford illustration.

Figure 6. The Drovers Arms: Basford illustration

2. Greece
The Greek team chose to celebrate 'Famous for a reason' by developing their own 360° campaign which integrated event sponsorship, on-trade, digital and PR activity.

The Grouse Trail
The Grouse Trail kicked off the 30-year celebrations in Greece with the commissioning of three contemporary designers to decorate The Grouse replicas, which were put on display at a range of events throughout the city. The Grouse statues were exhibited at The Ermis Awards (the biggest event rewarding creativity in the communications industry) in front of 1,500 delegates, including trendsetters and opinion formers in media, advertising and marketing.

They also presented the 125 award winners with personalised bottles put on display, reinforcing the "Famous for a reason" message. Branding in such a special and contemporary way ensured that The Famous Grouse "owned the event" and created a talking point.

The statues were then put on display at a range of functions by the team throughout the campaign. To generate further awareness and publicity around the campaign, two short films were uploaded to YouTube telling the story of The Grouse Trail.

The Famous 75 Bars

The second major part of the campaign was The Famous 75 Bars. In association with leading lifestyle publication *Athens Voice*, a digital campaign was created in which readers could celebrate and then vote for their favourite bars in Greece.

Athens Voice was celebrating reaching 50,000 Facebook friends and so the campaign kicked off with two parties (one in Athens and one in Salonica) which the publication hosted and were sponsored by The Famous Grouse. As an added twist and to mark The Famous Grouse's 30-years celebration, anyone born in 1980 could join the party for free. More than 2,500 people attended the parties and had the chance to sample The Famous Grouse drinks.

The next stage involved asking *Athen's Voice* readers to nominate which bars they felt deserved to be made "famous". Readers could nominate and leave comments about their favourite bar through an interactive Facebook application. To incentivise readers, competitions ran throughout the campaign. The result was a 10-page feature in *Athen's Voice* detailing the Top 75 Famous Bars in Athens.

CAUSE FOR CELEBRATION

Keeping anything going for thirty years these days is a major triumph. But to maintain a place at number one in the highly-competitive whisky industry is an extraordinary achievement. The Famous Grouse made the most of that feat from August 2010 to December 2011 worldwide with an impressive volley of events, promotions and campaigns, all geared towards explaining why the brand is 'Famous for a reason'. Extra spice was provided with a hearty cocktail of replica birds, social media and great bars that were 'Famous for a reason'.

The campaign delivered on all the original objectives as set out previously:

- Clearly convey the No.1 whisky in Scotland message in the warm and witty 'Grouse' tone of voice.
- Communicate the 'Famous for a reason' message.
- Increase reach and saliency among current consumers and reassure light buyers by giving them a reason to believe.
- To provide all markets with a clear 360° campaign that easily developed and delivered these objectives.

Most importantly, sales increased and grew the brand. Overall, despite the blended Scotch market only growing at an average of 1%, the brand grew by +8.31% between 2010/11 to 2011/12.

All images appearing in this case study are reproduced by permission of Edrington.

AXE
Global success through universal brand truths

SNAPSHOT
Unilever revitalised its Axe (Lynx) male grooming brand with an ingenious cross-border campaign for its new variant which gripped the imagination of its key consumers.

AGENCY
Bartle Bogle Hegarty

KEY INSIGHTS
- Unilever's Axe brand (Lynx in the UK) had built up a hugely-successful global franchise by becoming synonymous with giving young men an edge with girls.
- However, in 2009 and 2010 two new variants failed to emulate past winners and the brand was in danger of losing ground with its key target audience.
- Returning to the core brand promise of 'seduction' and finding a fresh and culturally-flexible way to communicate it unlocked significant value for Axe, boosting value and volume sales and creating a new generation of fans.

SUMMARY
The male deodorant spray Axe (known as Lynx in the UK and a few other countries) is one of the leading male grooming brands in the world. Owned by Unilever, it has long been famous for its proposition that it makes men irresistible to women: 'the Axe effect'.

Each year Axe launches a completely new fragrance, packaging and communications campaign to replace the cohort of young men that naturally graduate from the brand.

To ensure consistency and to maximise commercial efficiencies, all communications ideas and assets are created centrally. So the constant challenge has been to bring the Axe effect to life in a way that is fresh and relevant to the federation of 100 markets.

In 2008, Axe launched its most successful new variant of all time, the chocolate-scented Dark Temptation. However, two subsequent variant launches, Twist and Instinct had drastically failed to perform. The brand risked a lost generation of young males not experiencing the Axe effect that would leave a hole in the brand's fortunes for years to come. The brand urgently needed another 'global hit'.

It found the answer with a new variant called Excite, with the resulting campaign highlighting its ability to seduce even the most virtuous of girls, using angels as symbols of female chastity. This concept travelled well across countries with the campaign gaining record-level local market investment, leading to a year-on-year (YOY) increase in brand relevance and a significant return on investment.

A DELICATE BALANCING ACT

Axe (known as Lynx in the UK and a few other countries) is the world's leading male deodorant body spray. Over the last fifteen years it has become famous for giving young men the edge with girls. This promise of seduction has been underpinned by great fragrances and a compelling brand idea: 'the Axe effect'. The brand is tightly targeted at young men as they make the transition from boyhood to manhood. However, tight targeting comes at a cost.

By the age of 24, men are only half as likely to buy Axe as their younger brothers, meaning that as older men leave the brand, penetration will decline unless the brand can bring in a new cohort of users each year. Axe therefore experiences churn of around 10-15% annually.

To counteract this, a key strategy for recruitment has been to launch a completely new variant, packaging and communications campaign each year. The communications idea for each new variant is created centrally. It is vital that each of Axe's 100 markets adopt the campaign for each new variant launch to ensure that the brand has a consistent brand voice and identity across the globe. Commercially, this approach provides substantial cost efficiencies to the business. It helps create 'global hits', which results in cultural traction for the brand, driving market penetration, repeat purchase and the ability to charge a price premium.

But when it goes wrong, it is a painful miss. Poorly-performing variants are quickly overlooked by young men, they become heavily discounted and ultimately burden Axe with an underperforming variant for years.

To be successful, concepts must therefore build enthusiasm among the local markets, work across channels and bring the Axe effect to life in a fresh way. Doing all three is a tough brief.

BRAND HITS AND MISSES

In 2008, Axe had launched its most successful global hit of all time, Dark Temptation. However, two subsequent new variant launches – Twist and Instinct – were complete misses. Campaigns were losing relevance with young men and generating lower volume sales for the brand. Failure to reverse this trend risked leaving a hole in the brand's fortunes for years to come.

There were three key business objectives in the search for the variant that would prove to be the next global hit – and, if not on the scale of Dark Temptation, would be successful enough to create the base that would set the brand up for future success.
- To grow value sales, with an ambitious target.
- Reverse the brand volume decline to ensure long-term performance.
- Introduce a variant which would sell at a premium of 130 vs. the category.

Along with the business objectives there were also three communications goals:
- Inspire, excite and instil confidence in the federation of markets around the world.
- Drive relevance. This called for a fresh take on the Axe effect that would resonate with a new generation of young men, be motivating enough to create cultural traction and universal enough to cross boundaries.
- Increase penetration by bringing new users to the brand.

Returning to a global hit meant analysing past hits and misses. The last hit, Dark Temptation, had been so successful because it was novel, humorous, and rooted in a universal product truth: the ability to seduce girls by smelling good enough to eat.

Recent misses had attempted to emulate the success of Dark Temptation by basing their creative concept in fragrance-related ideas. For example, Instinct dramatised the leather attributes of the fragrance, while Twist was about its changing nature. But this approach had ceased to be compelling and the brand's relevance was declining accordingly.

FINDING A UNIVERSAL SYMBOL

The solution was to look beyond fragrance and remind men of the core brand truth that lay at the heart of the Axe effect: seduction. Although the brand promise remained constant, it was important to find a fresh, relevant and universal take on seduction. In recent years, the archetypal woman in teenage male fantasies had become an overtly sexy and 'easily' available woman: the 'naughty girl'. Pop star Shakira's 2010 smash hit 'She Wolf' was the embodiment of this. On the face of it, naughty girls were what young men were presumed to dream about. They appeared at the top of Google searches and were the subject of banter in classrooms across the globe.

However, making use of this idea presented a challenge for Axe since there was a limit to how far the brand could go. In a world where unlimited web pornography was the norm for the target audience, it would be difficult to create cut-through and at the same time please more conservative markets.

Global qualitative research with young men quickly produced an illuminating insight: despite talking a good game, the unspoken truth was that young men were relatively timid and inexperienced. The actual fantasy of an Axe guy was a 'nice girl'. They were closer to the girls that they knew in real life, and as such, less intimidating. This equated to a more realistic (hence motivating) promise of 'getting some'.

This led to building the strategy around the virtue young men found so attractive in 'nice girls' in order to give Axe the biggest possible role in their lives: the ability to seduce even the most virtuous of girls. The next step would be to bring this idea of virtue to life in a way that would be culturally relevant globally.

There were 'nice girl' archetypes in every culture. The challenge was finding a universal one. The creative leap came from focusing on the most iconic symbol of female virtue in history: angels.

Globally, angels were icons of innocence, purity, wholesomeness and 'virtue'. The concept of angels also offered a universally relevant visual language because angels feature not only in Christian, Jewish and Islamic traditions, but in Sikhism and new age philosophy as well. They also provided a vast quantity of assets such as wings, feathers, halos and gothic style type that would travel across global borders. The variant was then named 'Excite' to symbolise a fragrance that would excite even the nicest of 'nice girls' to forgo their virtue at the exposure of the Axe effect.

SOLVING THE GLOBAL/LOCAL EQUATION

To gain fame and cultural traction for the Angels campaign, a suite of assets would have to be created that would have a big impact in broadcast channels and encourage engagement.

- Creating fame. The embodiment of the 'angels' idea was captured in an epic 90-second film: *Even Angels Will Fall*, which depicted angels renouncing their virtues after succumbing to the seductive powers of the Axe effect (Figure 1). The story was also extended through a series of striking visuals in print and outdoor (Figure 2).
- Creating cultural traction. Various engagement platforms were used to give the audience personal experiences with the 'angels' that they could also share. Using Google Earth technology, they were able to tempt an 'angel' down from the sky to their own street. One of the very first iAds put angels at the young man's fingertips, allowing him to download the film and music track, as well as interact with the angels. In addition, the film's soundtrack – a special choral cover of Air's 'Sexy Boy' produced in collaboration with the band – was available for download via iTunes.

The creative concept was so strong that it could be easily adapted to encompass local cultural sensitivities without affecting the core idea. For example, in non-Christian regions the angels were altered to goddesses. Local markets got behind the idea with enthusiasm and invested in local activation to intensify the brand's impact in their

Figure 1. Axe 'Excite' film

markets. For example:

- In London commuters could see themselves interacting with the angels live on a big screen thanks to some innovative use of augmented reality.
- In Germany men could compete with each other for a 'real life' date with an angel.
- In Chile, angels were projected onto iconic buildings in Santiago.

Figure 2. Print campaign

WINNING ON EVERY FRONT

Axe Excite was the first 'global hit' since Dark Temptation. The campaign was so successful that it renewed local market confidence, connected with the target audience and became a cultural talking-point. It surpassed its commercial objectives and turned the brand's fortunes around.

1. Meeting communications objectives
- Drive brand relevance. The success of the campaign meant that brand relevance grew 11% vs. 2010, reversing a trend of decline.
- Increase penetration. Excite increased penetration, bringing 11.6% more male consumers into the brand than an average new variant.

2. Success for the variant
- Volume sales. Excite's first-year volume sales showed a significant increase on the previous two years, selling +35% more than Instinct or Twist.
- Price premium. A key business objective was to sell Excite at a premium. The variant achieved a price premium of 137 vs. the category, seven points more than the 130 target.
- Value sales. The first year's value sales showed a significant increase on those of previous years. As well as comparing favourably to other variants, Excite exceeded its ambitious sales target by 7.8%.

3. Overall brand benefits

- Reverse in brand volume decline. Excite reversed the trend of decline in total brand volume sales, creating total brand growth of 4.76%, attracting a cohort of new brand users.
- Brand value growth. Axe Excite grew overall brand value sales by +5.1% vs 2010, the first significant growth for four years.

4. Inspiring local markets

- The uptake of a new variant by markets is not a foregone conclusion. Major markets at times refuse to launch variants if they don't like the creative concept. Axe Excite ran in all 100 Axe markets.

5. Cultural relevance

- This fresh take on the Axe brand promise was relevant to young men globally. The concept of 'angels' did indeed resonate with the target audience's fantasies, as research suggested. Gaining cultural traction. Angels were a compelling topic of conversation for young men, driving them to engage with the brand in social channels. This drove buzz and raised the social profile of the brand. The 'angels ' became a global online cultural phenomenon.

6. Long-term payback

- Using actual data wherever possible, and projected data where necessary, three-year return on investment (ROI) can be calculated for each Axe new variant. Despite a higher media spend, Axe Excite proved to be the most profitable campaign since Dark Temptation, returning €2.36 for every €1 spent.

CHAPTER 7   07

Re-energising long
established brands

So here's the thing about brand revitalisation. It's the hardest challenge a marketer can take on. These cases are excellent examples of companies who have done it well. But, by their very nature, any single case oversimplifies what it takes to be successful.

You need a great campaign idea, as demonstrated by adam&eveDDB in the Foster's case. It has to recognise accurately current perceptions of the brand and take them head on.

You need a clear strategy rooted in economics that work. That was the gamble that National Lottery took. Doubling the price, and retaining consumer interest and frequency. No mean feat.

You need to understand the impact of word-of-mouth and how your brand fits into the cultural conversation. Jaguar faced the challenge of not only convincing its target audience, but also their friends and colleagues, to make it a highly-respected choice again.

And you need to activate with excellence at every touchpoint. That's the enormous challenge British Airways faced. Of course, Bartle Bogle Hegarty could come up with a great campaign. But to ensure that 'To fly. To serve.' was delivered in hundreds of millions of consumer interactions, each of whom would have had their own expectations of what that means – now that's something!

I hope as you read these cases, you think actively about not just the core strategies that drove each of them but what it would take to inspire whole organisations to deliver brand revitalisation.

Syl Saller
Chief Marketing Officer
Diageo Plc

FOSTER'S
Returning the brand to the glory days

SNAPSHOT
A light-hearted campaign that struck a deep chord with the target male audience saw Foster's climb back on top.

AGENCY
adam&eveDDB

KEY INSIGHTS
- The Foster's brand was languishing from a triple whammy of a lacklustre brand performance, a declining category and a shrinking market.
- A campaign combining Australian humour with portrayals of young men that resonated with the target group saw a significant reversal of fortunes.
- From the launch of the campaign in 2010 Foster's grew in both volume and value to retake the leading market position as younger drinkers flocked back to the brand.

SUMMARY
Heineken UK is one of the country's leading beer and cider businesses and the name behind iconic drinks brands such as Foster's, Strongbow, Bulmers, Heineken, Kronenbourg 1664 and Desperados, together with a full range of speciality brands.

However, back in 2010 the company was facing a formidable challenge with its Foster's lager brand. With the UK beer category in its sixth consecutive year of decline, lager volumes were shrinking faster than ever. While trying to fend off the advances of premium/world lager and modern cider, standard lager brands were also fighting each other for an ever-decreasing slice of the market. And to make matters worse, deep discounting by retailers had created a price compression that consumers were becoming used to.

If the marketplace wasn't treacherous enough, the Foster's brand was weak too. It had an incoherent proposition and an outdated personality. The icon of the 1980s had become tired, dusty and irrelevant. Turning the brand's fortunes around seemed a foreboding task.

Yet, at a time when drinkers were abandoning lager, Foster's created a change in consumer behaviour that increased both volume and value. Over three short years and against all the odds, Foster's bucked the market trend and reinvigorated the category. Producing some of the most effective and enjoyable marketing in the sector, Foster's long-term brand revitalisation truly connected with Britain's lager drinkers and quickly propelled the brand to number one.

TROUBLES MOUNT UP

In its heyday of the 1980s, the 'Amber Nectar' was both iconic and a powerhouse for delivering volume. However, by 2010, Foster's was in a state of 'double jeopardy': it was underperforming, and doing so in a category that was shrinking. In the face of a global financial crisis, it was a time of genuine doom and gloom.

Lager is big business. More than 6.4 million pints are sold in the UK every day. However in 2010, the British brewing industry was facing the toughest of times and the category was shrinking. Between 2004 and 2010, standard lager volumes had dropped by 18.5%, effectively wiping out 12 million hectolitres from the industry

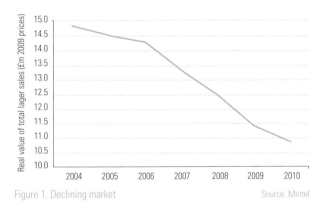

Figure 1. Declining market   Source: Mintel

(Figure 1). That was the equivalent of lager's top two brands total volume, combined. British blokes weren't drinking less, they were just drinking differently: premium beer, cider and spirits had grown in popularity, plus the growing acceptance of wine among men had meant that lagers were now being replaced with other types of alcoholic drinks. Brands like Foster's were now fighting with entirely different categories of alcoholic drinks for a share of consumption.

Despite being one of the most iconic lager brands of the 1980's, by the 2000's the Foster's brand had lost affinity with its core audience of 18-24 year old males. It was in a category going backwards within an underperforming sector and the weakened brand was losing share too (Figure 2).

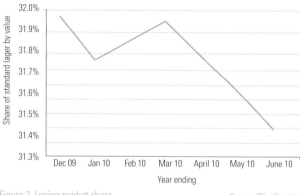

Figure 2. Losing market share   Source: IRI, off-trade

Foster's was an underperforming lager, in an underperforming category, in a shrinking market. Help was on the horizon in the form of a new premium variant – Foster's Gold. But Gold wasn't scheduled for release until late 2011. If the brand was to be a financial success, Foster's would not only need to increase its share of whatever was left of the standard lager marketplace, but it also had to strengthen the brand to pave the way for a successful launch of Foster's Gold.

THE NEW BATTLEGROUND

The economics of the beer industry are simple. Sell the biggest volume possible at the highest margin possible. Traditionally, beer brands would focus their efforts on pubs and clubs. However, by 2010 the tide had turned. Most consumption was now happening at home.

Since the 1980s, the increasing strength of the big supermarkets had been driving down off-trade prices. This, allied with less social acceptance of drink-driving and more stringent legislation, had led to a long-term trend towards off-premises consumption. And the recession only accelerated that trend. The young men who were Foster's core target were the engine room of the lager category. Their consumption was frequent and heavy, which is why they could be relied on to drive volume.

But they were increasingly avoiding the pub, choosing to save money by drinking at home. With an average of seven pubs closing a day in 2009, Foster's could no longer rely on them to drive volume. It was clear that the battleground had shifted: off-licenses and supermarkets was where the war needed to be won.

The big problem was that, by 2010, mainstream lager had become a 'sea of sameness'. There was little to separate the main players and consumers couldn't distinguish between either the brands, or the prices in their local off-licence. Foster's, Carling, Carlsberg and Stella seemed 'samey' to the public and retailers felt the same way too. With little to distinguish them, retailers saw lager brands as entirely substitutable, and would only offer support to whichever brand could offer them the lowest price per litre.

Brands were cycled through a discount 'merry-go-round' to stimulate sales. This retailer 'price compression' was killing all the mainstream lager margins, and Foster's needed to find a way to stand apart. Brands with strong affinity automatically create high levels of desirability, so they don't require discounting to drive sales volume. However, consumers felt little connection to the Foster's lager brand, and affinity scores were low. Foster's had lost its personality and had become as bland as the rest of the category.

TUNING IN TO THE AUDIENCE

The challenge was clear. Foster's needed to find differentiation within the lager category that would make it an active 'off-trade' choice for Britain's young lager drinkers.

Launched in the UK in the 1980's, Foster's lager was a brand built upon 'Australian heritage'. Despite being brewed in Manchester, the brand's communications featured the quintessentially antipodean Paul Hogan, who epitomised the laid-back and carefree attitude that was befitting to the Aussie stereotype of the time. Foster's commercials featuring Hogan were among the nation's favourites, with the infamous 'Ballet' spot being recognised as one of Britain's most-loved commercials in a Channel 4 poll.

This affinity for the brand directly translated into sales. But times had changed. Post the Hogan era, Foster's struggled to capture the nation's imagination in quite the same way. Despite some memorable marketing moments, (such as 'Think, Drink') over the course of two decades, the brand's affinity scores slipped, and sales had ebbed away.

To get more young Brits to engage with Foster's, the brand needed to be more relevant, while unlocking a compelling side of its Australian heritage. However, the 'ideal' that was Australia had lost its lustre. The tyranny of distance that had once kept the 'Great Southern Land' shrouded in a glorious mystique was no longer a reality. Thousands of Brits had actually travelled to and experienced Australia for themselves.

"Oz" was filled with deserts, deadly land and sea creatures and it also had an ugly side. Sydney's Cronulla riots proved that Australians weren't sun-kissed surf gods; they were dumb, drunk and racist. And to top it all off, they weren't even better at cricket any more.

Getting under the skin of Foster's target, who were identified as 'tribal drinkers', it became apparent how disassociated they felt from modern marketing (see box: Getting under their skin'). They felt unequivocally that no commercial portrayals of men were accurate and that 'blokes were being beaten up' by both the media and marketing. In short, they didn't see anything of themselves reflected in brand communications.

An extensive research project into the lives of 'tribal drinkers' was seen as key to revitalising the brand. And, perhaps unsurprisingly, the answer came from the most traditional of methods: eavesdropping. In 'riding along' with tribal drinkers, two key insights emerged:

- They lived for the camaraderie of Friday and Saturday. For a few hours every weekend, they could truly 'be themselves' in the spontaneous environments that being with their mates created. They were a positive bunch and were filled with the optimism that 'any time with their mates had the potential to be the best time of their lives'.
- They had more issues to deal with. On the cusp of breaking into manhood, tribal drinkers were growing up and starting to face some of life's trickier social dilemmas. Leaving home, getting serious in a relationship and increasing work responsibility were of concern to them. It was noticed that among the banter and fun, other tribal drinkers were both a support group and sounding board for how to deal with these issues.

GETTING UNDER THEIR SKIN
The 'Great male survey' in 2009 from Askmen.co.uk revealed just how disassociated young men felt from modern marketing when asked: "What portrayal of men in TV commercials is the most accurate?"

11%	"The fumbling boyfriend/husband"
13%	"The beer-swigging party guy"
67%	"No commercial portrayals of men are accurate"

The best beer advertising does one simple thing: it gives an emotional free sample of the brand. With this in mind, the tension between these insights posed the potential solution: could Foster's help soothe the insecurities of the tribal drinker?

RECAPTURING THE BRAND'S ESSENCE
Foster's core equity was that it's Australian. However, it was no secret that Foster's wasn't made there, or even drunk there now, although it had started being exported from the country of its origins back in the early 1970s. And tribal drinkers were quick to point out that the best part of Australia is the attitude it has always 'exported': a laid-back, no-worries sense of positivity.

This attitude was compelling to the audience, reflecting the positivity they saw in themselves and was an equity the brand could actively leverage. If tribal drinkers were using social drinking occasions to assuage themselves of their angst and issues, then Foster's now had permission to help out with its uniquely Australian attitude and perspective.

Figure 3. 'Good Call' campaign

The creative solution was to create an 'umbilical cord' between Brits and their Aussie cousins. Using a long distance call between tribal drinkers and their Australian counterparts, Foster's would provide guidance, some sunshine and a positive outlook to men's dilemmas. Launched on TV, through Facebook and with a regular 'Dilemma' column in *Shortlist* magazine, the 'Good Call' campaign was born (Figure 3).

The target group's response to ads was overwhelmingly positive. By the end of 2011, Nielsen scored Foster's 'Haircut' as the sixth most liked ad of the year, the only beer commercial to make the top ten. Additionally, Foster's was a top trending topic on Twitter for six weeks. YouTube views had an average 96% like rating, and the positive comments eloquently reflected this.

The communications also changed people's response to the brand. The Net Promoter Score rose to more than double that of Carling (Millward Brown 2011) and brand recall surpassed not only lager rivals Carlsberg and Stella Artois, but also cider brand Magners and the ever-present Guinness as well.

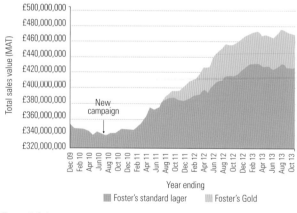

Figure 4. Sales soar

Source: IRI, off-trade

A BRAND BACK ON TOP

From the start of 'Good Call', sales immediately lifted, and continued to do so. Even when Foster's Gold was launched, over a year later, sales of the standard lager kept on growing. The brand had re-established its strength, and was massively outperforming its competitors. It was the only standard lager in growth, bucking the category trend (Figures 4 and 5).

Sales growth 2009-2013

	Change in Sales value	Change in Sales volume
Foster's	+20%	+7%
Carling	-1%	-13%
Carlsberg	-3%	-14%
Stella	-24%	-34%
Total market	+3%	-9%

Figure 5. Leading the pack   Source: IRI. Standard lagers, off trade

The appeal of Foster's also began to help recruit drinkers into lager. Of all mainstream lager brands, Foster's was seen to be the most attractive lager brand for younger drinkers switching into lager (Alcovision 2010). Figure 6 illustrates the brand's significant growth in popularity and appeal.

Significant equity measure growth

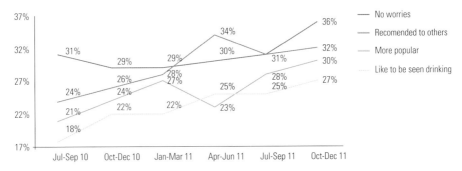

Figure 6. Brand appeal

Tribal drinkers lapped up the work and the product in equal measure. In the three years from when 'Good Call' began in 2010, Foster's grew from third place in the offtrade market, to first in both volume and value.

With tribal drinkers actively seeking out Foster's, retailers began to realise the value in the brand too. Rather than using discounting to fund growth, Foster's did the opposite. Under the momentum of increasing sales growth, Foster's was actually able to increase its price per litre above the standard lager average, clearly indicating the brand's renewed strength.

All images appearing in this case study are reproduced by permission of Foster's.

BRITISH AIRWAYS
Reigniting brand confidence

SNAPSHOT
A radical marketing strategy that embraced both internal and external audiences helped restore the brand's fortunes.

AGENCY
Bartle Bogle Hegarty

KEY INSIGHTS
- Over the last decade the British Airways brand had been under pressure from severe market upheaval.
- It decided to mount a vigorous campaign based on a marketing master plan which was centred on its core ethos of 'To fly. To serve.' and covered every touchpoint.
- Well aware that as a service brand success would stem from staff engagement, BA targeted its internal audience as firmly as its customers with the refreshed brand message.
- The result has been steady growth in key success measurements, including an enhanced profile through its social media presence.

SUMMARY
The last decade had been a time of enormous change for the airline industry. For the UK's flagship airline, British Airways (BA), it had meant focusing on restructuring the business, transforming its operations and, more recently, entering into strategic relationships with other airlines.

By 2010 the time was ripe for revitalising the brand's relationship with customers. This centred on a comprehensive campaign to underline its commitment to its core ethos: 'To fly. To serve.' The starting point was to put service back at the heart of the business. This was bolstered by an integrated campaign spanning TV, social media and print, while a film was created to win both internal and external backing for the

'To fly. To serve.' message. To ensure that it struck the right note, it featured those who embodied the culture: BA pilots.

Other elements included documentaries with customers, extensive blogging, outdoor ads and print. By 2012, with the arrival of the London Olympics, thanks to these internal and external efforts, BA was ready to take its place as the official airline partner with pride. More significantly, improved brand and revenue performance measures continue to reflect the success of the campaign.

FACING TESTING MARKET CHALLENGES

BA spent the majority of the 20th century leading the commercial aviation industry since its early beginnings when it operated as Imperial Airways. The airline was instrumental in helping pioneer the technology needed to make global air travel a viable reality while acting as a torchbearer for premium customer service in the air. From the British royal family to famous UK footballers, everyone chose to fly the airline (Figure 1).

Figure 1. Leading the industry

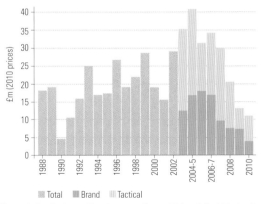

Total Brand Tactical

Figure 2. Tactical spending rises   Source: Nielsen & ZenithOptimedia

However, from 2001 there had been a series of external and internal challenges that took the world-class airline from leadership to a fierce competitive battle for consumers' hearts and minds. Not only did the airline face increasing competition from an evolving category of lower-cost competitors who were challenging its short-haul European routes, but foreign premium airlines were squeezing the brand's global long-haul network.

By 2010 the company was at a crossroads: continue to chase short-term sale revenues with tactical brand expenditure (Figure 2) or take a step back and figure out how to be a leader again by reminding customers of the brand's strengths. The result was its first major brand campaign in more than ten years.

GETTING THE AIRLINE BACK ON TRACK
The company began to prepare for its comeback by embarking on Project Flight Path, which aimed to uncover those areas where the brand could claim leadership. It went back to basics, asking questions such as:
- Who should the brand be targeting?
- What is the airline's brand difference?
- What are the must-win battles?

The answers showed that flyers still had a latent love for the brand, and that the brand's core foundations remained intact: passion and expertise for flying coupled with human, 'British' service.

This helped determine the three pillars of strength (Figure 3) for the BA brand:
- Superior flying know-how
- Thoughtful service
- British style

Superior flying know-how	Thoughtful service	British style
• 90 years of flying heritage	• Service that is warm	• Understated design elegance
• Pilots recognised as the best in the world	• Recognises and respects individuals	• Champions of contemporary British style and talent
• Safety and engineering setting world standards	• Staff are trained to handle any situation	• Partnering with the best of Britain
• Innovation that makes travel seamless		

Figure 3. Three pillars of strength   Source: Project Flight Path

MARKETING RENAISSANCE

The challenge for the company's agency, Bartle Bogle Hegarty (BBH), was to take these learnings and bring them to life through an idea that would put the brand back on a leading path (See: 'A manifesto for the brand's rebirth').

The result was a long-term, three-step approach to execute 'To fly. To serve.' in order to build confidence and commitment and regain leadership. First, the idea of 'To fly. To serve.' had to be given meaning. The ethos had strong provenance, having once been painted on all the airline's aircraft and was still stitched into every crew member's jacket and every pilot's hat. If brought to life at every touchpoint, this ethos would have the potential to reignite the brand's leadership ambitions (Figure 4).

Figure 4. 'To fly. To serve.' crest   Source: BA/For People

The three steps would then encompass the key elements for revival: colleagues, customers and culture. Restoring colleague morale and putting service back into the heart of the business would be critical. With the staff on board the airline could reach out to customers and, through successive marketing campaigns with the opportunity of the Olympics in London in 2012, reassert itself firmly back into contemporary culture.

1. Engagement strategy

An engagement strategy was created to affect the turnaround. It would reach out first to colleagues who would then help deliver it to customers. It was important to develop a series of assets that appealed simultaneously both to the internal and external audience (Figure 5). It started with making 'To fly. To serve.' a visible commitment by painting it back onto the planes.

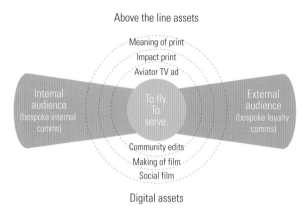

Figure 5. Engagement strategy.   Source: BBH

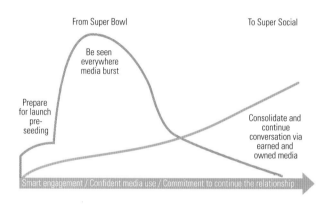

Figure 6. Super Bowl/Super Social media engagement strategy   Source: BBH

2. Media strategy

It had been ten years since BA had been involved with brand-led marketing. The airline needed a big impact to get its brand message across to customers and demonstrate to staff that the brand was again aiming for the top.

In 2011 yoghurt maker Yeo Valley and BBH described how they had employed a 'Super Bowl/Super Social' media engagement strategy. For this relaunch campaign, BBH took this further with a Super Bowl/Super Social Plus campaign strategy (Figure 6).

3. The campaign

A film was then created to act as the heart and soul and to align internal and external audiences with the new ethos. It was essential that it was representative of the people who would live it: the BA staff. 'Aviators', a 90" and 60" film, featured thirteen BA employees and focused on the most iconic examples of 'To fly. To serve.': BA pilots.

A number of steps followed:
- Step one: re-engage with an internal audience.
  BA staff members were the first to be shown the film and be engaged in presentations held at the brand's hub, Heathrow's Terminal 5. At these sessions the company announced a five-year, £5 billion reinvestment plan. The company was announcing its plans to get back on top, to empower its staff and put the customer back at the heart of the business. After years of aggressive cost-cutting, the brand was now committing the business to regaining leadership.

A MANIFESTO FOR THE BRAND'S REBIRTH

"In a situation like this there is no point in promising something the brand cannot deliver. No point making claims that the customer can easily refute through their own experiences. No point hiding behind a glossy ad campaign that simply attempts to paper over the cracks. This is a moment in time when an airline must speak about itself. And for itself.

We need to reach back inside the brand in the knowledge that we are seeking the rebirth of a brand, not just the creation of the next ad campaign. To do that we have to find the fundamental truths that remain alive in British Airways, even if dulled by events of the last few years. Truths that can resonate not only with the customer but also help re-energise a disillusioned and demotivated staff.

For, at the end of the day, British Airways' product is its people. Deep down in British Airways still lie the values of expertise and passion. What has and still does define British Airways is its passion and unrivalled expertise for flying and commitment to making the experience special for everyone.

It is that expertise, built over decades and generations, that lies at the heart of the deep trust we believe still exists for British Airways, notwithstanding all the problems of recent times. These are the values and truths that need reigniting. We make no apology for proposing the return to centre stage of the four words that are, as we have said before, literally stitched into the fabric of the airline. Words that capture so succinctly the truths we are talking about: To fly. To serve."

Nigel Bogle, BBH, 24th February 2011

- Step two: re-engage with the external audience.
  The next step was to reconnect with passionate flyers. These brand loyalists, properly engaged, would help promote the brand during the Super Bowl launch and act as brand advocates during the Super Social phase. This was the first step for the brand to take to rebuild its connection to customers.

  Footage from the 90" film was re-cut into seven separate films and combined with bespoke footage and interviews from behind-the-scenes. These short documentaries were seeded prior to campaign launch. Each film was aimed at a specific consumer group who still felt strongly about the airline and its history. A dedicated blogger team contacted each group and built a relationship, sharing the films and exclusive information about the forthcoming launch.

- Step three: campaign launch.
  The campaign TV ad was unveiled on the 21st of September 2011. It was first premiered on the brand's Facebook page at 11am, followed by the TV premiere on Channel 4 that evening. The launch film was supported by outdoor and press assets to help create greater impact around 'To fly. To serve.'. Figure 7 shows examples of the press activity designed to demonstrate the airline's total commitment to its manifesto.

Figure 7. Campaign press assets   Source: BBH

- Step four: sustaining the campaign.
  Ads focusing on what the ethos meant followed on from those geared to creating maximum impact. These ads were designed to avoid airline category clichés by showing BA service benefits through staff-led brand truths.

On the digital platform online films told more in-depth stories of the people who lived the brand values. For example, 'Kite Surfer' was the story of a BA pilot and world champion kite surfer, emphasising her passion and commitment to flying. 'Africa Relief' followed the story of the BA volunteer team as they transported a plane load of UNICEF aid from Europe to East Africa and back in under 24 hours.

GOING FOR OLYMPIC GOLD

From the outset, BA was determined to restore the passion and pride among its staff and lay the groundwork for the airline to move into the Olympic year as official airline partner, with momentum and confidence as a once-in-a-lifetime opportunity. The 'We're Ready' campaign was the company's demonstration of 'To fly. To serve.' through an Olympic lens. The £5 billion reinvestment into the business was beginning to bear fruit and, with talk of chaos and upheaval in the lead-up to the Games, the airline wanted to communicate the fact that it could perform beyond expectations.

In print, the airline talked about the capabilities of its staff serving the equivalent of three Olympic-sized pools worth of tea on board, and laying enough cable in new aircraft to cover an Olympic track eighty times. On TV BA wanted to demonstrate the readiness of the one part of the business customers were most disappointed with: the baggage crews.

During this period BA also unveiled multiple brand improvements to enhance customer service, including the food and an improved Executive Club (Figure 8).

Figure 8. Customer service brand improvements   Source: BBH & Ogilvy

Having engaged customers through its Olympic warm-up campaign, BA now asked what 'To fly. To serve.' demanded of the airline as the Olympic Games approached: 'What could BA do to demonstrate it is the most patriotic supporter of Team GB?' The airline was aware that to achieve this it needed an idea that reached out not only to customers but also to the culture itself.

The momentum from its new ethos gave the company enough confidence to develop an idea so bold that it would guarantee cultural relevance for it during the Games. The 'Don't fly' campaign gave BA a legitimate role to play in the Games by enabling it to command a new, confident tone in communications while it was directing all activity into supporting and spurring on the home athletics team. To the tune of the Clash's 'London Calling', BA physically taxied people from the airport to the Games, while online BA let people get involved by taking a BA plane down their street (Figure 9).

Figure 9. 'Don't fly' campaign   Source: BBH

Meanwhile, in print, BA rallied the nation to show its support for the teams and exploit the home advantage. A wide array of different activities were carried out during both the Olympics and Paralympics games, including sponsoring ParkLive at the Olympic Park and running daily reactive press ads supporting the athletes.

ENJOYING BRAND RENEWAL

1. Re-connecting with colleagues

The first step of the brand relaunch was to re-engage colleagues. BA needed to re-establish morale and a sense of purpose among its 36,000 staff. The 'To fly. To serve.' kick-started this objective, with eight out of 10 employees reporting that they were proud to work for BA. With each wave of successive activity, the morale of the staff continued to grow to new heights in step with the brand's renewed marketing confidence. After just over the two years of the initiative:

- 91% said they were proud to work for BA.
- 87% said working for BA made them want to do the best they could.
- 92% were confident that BA would be successful in the future.
- 87% would speak highly of BA's products.
- 67% would speak highly of BA's customer service.
- 71% would recommend BA as a great place to work.

2. Focusing on customers

Brand measures that looked at customer perceptions of the airline rose significantly after 'To fly. To serve.' and continued to rise with each successive campaign. 'Desire', a BA brand metric that tracks customer choice when price is removed, saw strong growth with each brand campaign. In addition, the brand's key success measurement, 'bonding' also rose year on year. So, while it had taken ten years for the brand to slip on this measure from 30% to 10%, in the space of twelve months there was a 5% rise.

3. Culture

With the launch of 'To fly. To serve.' the airline's social media presence increased in significance, contributing to its reconnected role in culture. Independent bodies confirmed this, with YouGov judging BA to be the UK's favourite airline (Figure 10).

Meanwhile, BA enjoyed successive periods of sustained growth from the campaign's inception, with month-on-month rises in revenue since 2010 (Figure 11).

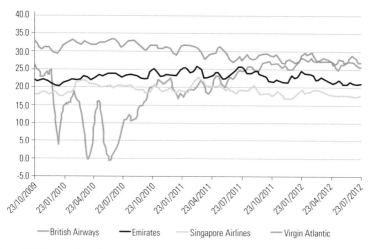

Figure 10. UK's favourite airlines

Source: YouGov

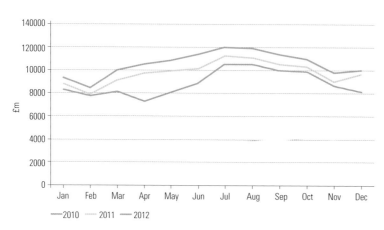

Figure 11. BA month by month revenue

Source: IAGshares.com

All images appearing in this case study are reproduced by permission of British Airways.

NATIONAL LOTTERY
Putting the brand back into play

SNAPSHOT
The National Lottery's bold marketing strategy not only returned the nation's biggest contributor to good causes back to growth but persuaded the public to accept a doubling of the price.

AGENCY
AMVBBDO

KEY INSIGHTS
- The National Lottery had to take some drastic action in the face of declining revenues as consumer engagement with its core Lotto game decreased.
- A carefully-crafted plan to reinvigorate the games, underpinned by extensive research and supported with a comprehensive and carefully-timed promotional campaign, was geared to injecting excitement back into a consumer product which had remained unchanged in nearly 20 years and convincing the public it was worth paying more to play.
- Taking such a risk paid off handsomely, with a substantial rise in weekly takings and an injection of new energy into the brand.

SUMMARY
The UK's National Lottery, run by Camelot, is one of the most successful lotteries in the world and the most cost-effective one in Europe, with only around 4% of total revenue spent on operating costs. In operating The National Lottery, Camelot delivers on average over £33 million each week to National Lottery good causes. Combined with Lottery Duty it pays to the government, Camelot returns one of the highest percentages of lottery revenue back to society in the world.

However, over time, while the National Lottery was growing as a whole, its core Lotto game had lost its sparkle and players were taking part more out of habit than because of active engagement. This was of national concern, as the lottery exists for one purpose only: to generate money for National Lottery good causes, supporting community, arts, sport, heritage and film projects across the country.

So the company which runs the lottery, Camelot, was determined to reinvigorate the game for its long-term health and to benefit the causes the game supports. This took nearly two years of careful development and a vast programme of player research and co-creation. The result was a £2 game (double the existing price), with enhanced smaller prizes, bigger jackpots and a brand new guaranteed Lotto raffle.

To overcome potential consumer resistance in a challenging financial environment the right go-to-market strategy and communications plan was critical. The ensuing multi-layered campaign using every owned, earned, shared and paid-for channel to create excitement and interest not only re-engaged players but saw revenues grow by a third.

FACING SOME HARD TRUTHS

The UK National Lottery was launched in 1994 with a single game, later renamed Lotto. It was created to generate money for good causes for the benefit of the nation. It gripped everyone's imagination, with 92% of adults playing for the very first jackpot of £5.8 million (which is equivalent to £9.77 million today).

As with every similar lottery around the world, a sales spike at the beginning (bigger in the UK than in any other country), was followed by a gradual but sustained decline in sales. By 2009, 68% of adults were playing (still a remarkable marketing achievement in itself, as most other national lotteries lose far more players).

The game's credentials are impressive. Lotto remains the nation's favourite game, while its logo is recognisable by 95% of the population. Lotto is also the UK's single-biggest fast-moving consumer goods (FMCG) brand (Figure 1). Over the last 20 years, it has given out over 800 million prizes (over 800,000 each week), made 3,203 millionaires and raised over £19 billion for good causes.

But while overall National Lottery sales (including EuroMillions and National Lottery Instants) had been in healthy growth for the past five years, Lotto was in steady decline (Figure 2). While a marketing strategy of product diversification had been very

2013 sales – Lotto vs UK's biggest grocery brands

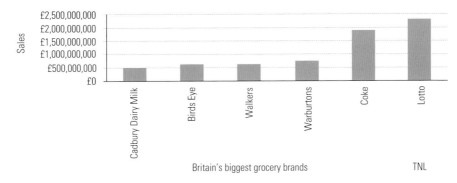

Figure 1. UK's biggest FMCG brand
Source: 'National Lottery Commission Annual Report and Accounts 2012/2013' and 'Nielsen: 52 w\e 04 January 2014'

Lotto sales since launch

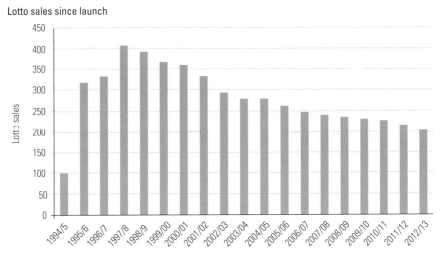

Figure 2. Declining sales (1994/5 indexed at 100)
Source: The National Lottery, Camelot UK Lotteries and Macro Consumer and Market Trends

successful and the excitement of the other games had captured players' imaginations and spend, Lotto had remained unchanged.

In order to understand the need for reinvigoration, it is important to understand how Lotto works.

Every week players contribute as much money to National Lottery good causes – £35 million – as Children In Need raises in a year. As the core National Lottery game, Lotto in particular matters so much because it raises around 50% of all the money that the National Lottery returns to good causes across its entire portfolio of games. Declining Lotto sales meant less money returned to the nation. This couldn't be allowed to continue. However, while the time was right to make changes, it had to be done in a particularly challenging tough economic climate.

ASKING ALL THE RIGHT QUESTIONS
Research revealed some hard truths:
- Players felt that Lotto had become boring.
- They were playing more out of habit than enjoyment.

The game does not exist without the players. The jackpots rise and fall depending on how many people play the game and how much money they put in (this is called the pari-mutuel system). In a pari-mutuel lottery game, there is at least one fixed prize tier, but the jackpot, and other prizes, are determined by the amount of money spent on tickets for each draw. This puts all players in mutual dependency, as they create the jackpots that some of them then win.

Since 1994, a one-line entry into the game had cost just £1. Adding excitement back by changing the prize structure to have more appealing prizes would mean growing the prize fund. And, in order to offer a meaningful change in prizes, that would mean changing the ticket price.

The marketing team created a range of different scenarios and price points and put them to the test. The new game was in development for 24 months in a test, learn, refine and repeat cycle. 140 concepts were tested in a quantitative study among 26,000 respondents and 70 research groups.

The resulting winning concept for new Lotto offered more chances to win more money. The £2 price per line would buy players entry to a game where matching three numbers would win them £25 (rather than £10) and a new Lotto raffle would create 50 winners of a guaranteed £20,000 in every draw, in addition to bigger jackpots (Figure 3). The £20,000 prize tier had been created in response to the research that showed players loved the idea of winning an amount that would change their lives in simple but meaningful ways, like paying for a wedding, university or school tuition fees or the deposit on a house.

The original £1 Lotto game ticket vs the new £2 Lotto ticket

Figure 3. The new game

This new game was preferred in research to a simple 'double the jackpot' concept, as it resolved the persistent feedback from players that they also wanted the lower prize tiers to be worth more. The new game concept had everything, and, while research indicated that there could be a potential loss of between 10-20% of players by raising the price, most players would like the changes being made, with some adjusting their spending to suit their wallet. Research also showed that the result would be a significant overall revenue increase, securing higher jackpots and ensuring an increase in valuable funds to good causes.

PLOTTING A CAREFUL COURSE

Making new Lotto happen in the real world would be an entirely different challenge. Commentators predicted a drastic fall in sales (Figure 4). A *Daily Express* headline claimed that the 'National Lottery price hike will cut ticket sales by 50%'. While the game could be planned in a quantitative study, putting it in the public domain under the scrutiny of news organisations and social media channels could attract some negative comment which would focus on the price rise fairly quickly.

Figure 4. Dire warnings

A strategy was devised to announce the game change nine months in advance of the launch to eradicate any risk that the story could leak and put the company on the back foot. By announcing the changes on its own terms, Camelot could manage it as positively as possible and minimise reputational damage as much as possible. It would allow plenty of time to explain the benefits, not just the price rise, and communicate the positive aspects of the changes to consumers.

The second part of the strategy was to leave no-one behind by bringing as many players as possible to the new version of the game. Any individual might choose to reduce spend, playing fewer 'lines', but, if they were still in the game, the relationship would be maintained and the benefits of the game over time would encourage them to play more. So those benefits needed to be very clear.

In the summer of 2013 the biggest retailer engagement campaign since the launch of The National Lottery in 1994 began with the training of 250,000 retail staff across 37,000 outlets. This campaign included a special retailer game just before the launch to ensure their full buy-in. For the launch itself, 23 million pieces of point-of-sale material were distributed and implemented across the retail base (Figure 5).

The scale of this effort cannot be under-estimated. The lottery organisers achieved a scale and level of implementation comparable to a large supermarket retailer but without owning any outlets or employing any of the people responsible for displaying the material. Substantial effort was put into helping retailers help Lotto succeed for the nation and their own bottom lines through increased retailer commission.

Figure 5. No retailer left behind

PROFITABLE PARTNERSHIPS
The communication platform "game-changing, life-changing" ran through everything, from the catchy TV advertising (which communicated the benefits of the new game both to players and to society), through to dramatic use of outdoor, radio, print, digital, social media and point-of-sale. Other elements included specially-built posters, a syndicate game on Facebook, a social media competition to 'sing-a-long' to the TV tune and floating giant Lotto balls down the Thames. In fact,

the TV advertising was so catchy that Manchester United fans used the tune to create a hymn to their new teenage prodigy Adnan Janusaj.

The media and communications plan involved an unprecedented level of investment in partnerships with newspapers and radio stations. Reader and listener promotions ran across every national newspaper title and regional newspaper group. Lotto became the first brand to give away £500,000 through all commercial radio stations, simultaneously, working with all four major commercial radio sales houses, Global, Bauer, Talksport and Absolute. This created a media-first syndicated listener promotion with 69 UK radio stations. It not only galvanised the whole industry behind a common goal but also equated to a value of +97% in additional on-air value vs. investment.

Bespoke promotions were developed for each of the major national and regional newspapers and news media groups. A great example was the *Sun*+Lotto, an exclusive offer of a 'second chance' Lotto raffle for the *Sun*'s digital readership (Figure 6). This both drove the newspaper's digital circulation and gave Lotto exposure across its media products. *Evening Standard* readers were even offered a flight into space.

Figure 6. Partnering with the *Sun*

The partnership approach gained Camelot particular privileges, like being able to print 1,000 unique winning raffle numbers overnight, in order to hit first editions following the launch draw. This contributed over £9 million in additional media value.

The draw show on BBC One was revamped and reinvented, adding excitement and a fresh look to the broadcast efforts, with Chris Evans as the new face of the show to ensure that the new game launched with a real bang (Figure 7). For the first two new Lotto draws there was a guaranteed £10 million jackpot and 1,000 guaranteed £20,000 raffle winners. The objective was to gain mass trial of the game through eye-catching promotions.

Figure 7.The new show

A WINNING RESULT

The launch of new Lotto was one of the boldest marketing moves in recent years, with a brand doubling its price and yet prospering as a result. This was a risky move with high stakes since, if it didn't work, then funds to vital good causes could have collapsed overnight.

But, thanks to meticulous research, planning and testing of the new game, this didn't happen. In fact, one of the greatest tributes to the marketing behind this change was how little negative media coverage was received at the time or in year-end round-ups. This was a smooth transition with some rather striking results for the brand.

- Sales revenue increased by 30% by the end of 2013.
- Almost 95% of players had continued playing.
- The tracking data showed that more than 80% of players said that new Lotto was easy to understand and play, with raffle awareness peaking at 79% (Figure 8).
- By the end of 2013 New Lotto had given almost 10 million prizes including 5,270 raffle winners and 30 millionaires.
- New Lotto continues to generate hundreds of millions of extra money for good causes.

High levels of awareness

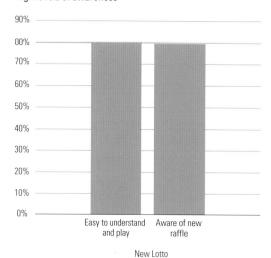

Figure 8. High levels of awareness

All images appearing in this case study are reproduced by permission of Camelot.

JAGUAR F-TYPE
The re-emergence of an iconic brand

SNAPSHOT
The car maker's global marketing campaign for its new sporty model not only saw it successfully establish itself in a new market segment but revitalised what had been a declining brand.

AGENCIES
Spark44, Mindshare, Brooklyn Brothers

KEY INSIGHTS
- Once one of the world's best-known and most desirable car brands, Jaguar's status had slipped as newer drivers deserted it for other high-volume premium marques such as BMW and Audi.
- That changed dramatically with a new multi-platform crossborder campaign built around its first new sporty model in over 40 years, the F-Type.
- The campaign not only increased interactions with the brand both in social channels and in real life test-drives but grew overall brand sales to outpace the category.

SUMMARY
Jaguar has been involved in the motor industry since its founding in the UK in 1922. It achieved worldwide status as a British icon after the second world war with a series of elegant and highly-desirable sports cars such as the E-Type. However, over time its fortunes had fluctuated as it moved through a variety of owners, including a short time in the late 1980s as an independent business, before being bought by Tata Motors in 2008.

During the last few years it had seen sales slow as competition in the high-volume premium car market intensified and its positioning became unclear. So it was determined to use its new F-Type convertible to spearhead revitalisation of the brand by creating desire for the entire range among a new generation of buyers. Taking a bold approach as it entered the sports car segment for the first time in 40 years, Jaguar issued a seductive invitation with intriguing content, celebrity PR, convincing communications and targeted media in partnership with Spark44 (brand strategy and communications), Mindshare (media and channel strategy) and Brooklyn Brothers (PR).

This allowed Jaguar to both meet and exceed its targets, with total volume growth of over 50% in China and 15% in the UK, the US, and Germany, a doubling of online configurations and a similar rise in test-drive requests. The company also outpaced average competitive sales in every market by at least 50% but with 10% or less share of voice. Importantly, it lifted employee morale at Jaguar and within the retail networks.

TAKING A DEFIANT STANCE

After a series of owners, Tata Group bought Jaguar from Ford in 2008. Good products were introduced but inadequate plans meant that while new models were praised by the industry, sales disappointed. In fact, with the exception of China, Jaguar's four-year average sales were down in key markets. Poor sales meant poor morale for employees and for the network of retailers. Losing confidence, retailers pushed staff, investment, and prospective buyers towards other brands.

Drivers had lost touch with the brand. In Western markets, Jaguar's image had decayed since the 1960s when Jaguar and the E-Type model embodied the essence of 'cool'. People still knew Jaguar's name, but not its current positioning or models. In China, where the brand was less than a decade old, awareness was also high but consideration low. Global research showed that despite awards for quality and solid industry reviews, poor product quality perceptions persisted. It also revealed that people generally perceived Jaguar as simply 'an old man's car'. This irrelevant image shut out new buyers, further ageing the driver base and worsening the problem.

Jaguar still defiantly believed it could reclaim a place as a high-volume premium automotive player. It made a brave decision to start brand transformation with a convertible sports car rather than a volume sedan. On paper it made little sense. But Jaguar believed the F-Type, its first true sports car in over 40 years, could be the catalyst for changing perceptions, channelling past glory to inject modernity and emotion into the brand (Figure 1).

Jaguar faced enormous challenges and great expectations heading up to the launch of the F-Type. A small player in the luxury automotive category, Jaguar needed the new

Figure 1. Launching the new F-Type

model to win in its own segment and lift the range overall. Focusing efforts on the top four markets of China, Germany, the UK, and the US, Jaguar was determined to create a campaign to create unprecedented desire for the brand and category-beating sales growth for the entire business.

This was a now-or-never moment, so Jaguar set decidedly ambitious goals across the range in order to force new methods and thinking from marketing.

1. Business objectives. Use the F-Type as a halo to increase overall global sales volume, outpacing the category in each country, specifically looking for 50% growth in China and 15% each in Germany, the US and the UK.

2. Behavioural and attitudinal goals. Intrigue sufficient numbers to fill the top-funnel metrics for future Jaguar consideration.
- Increase engagement with Jaguar websites with three metrics. Different budgets meant individually-defined goals.
  - Increase overall unique visits. Specifically, China needed to double its volume, Germany by +30%, the USA +20% and the UK +5% (home market traffic was already strong).
  - All markets to increase online car configurations by 50%.
  - All markets to double online test-drive requests.
- Get Jaguar into the conversation by making the brand relevant through public relations (PR), events, and social activity.
  - China: press reach of three million.
  - Germany: press reach of three million and get 5,000 registered users on F-Type Circle, a social/customer relationship management (CRM) digital program.
  - UK: press reach of 25 million and rank in the top five brands for Facebook post-engagement rates.
  - USA: press reach of 750 million impressions and reach one million Facebook 'likes'.

FACING THE REALITIES

An analysis of both primary and secondary research, including numerous in-market product clinics and focus groups, revealed that the biggest barrier to purchase was 'permission to buy'. People had latent goodwill for Jaguar, and, when directly confronted with the current brand and products, both younger audiences and those in new markets found the British design, performance, and innovation appealing compared to the dominant German brands. Even if they liked the cars, however, Jaguar remained a 'risky' choice that would need justifying to friends and colleagues. This was the exact opposite of what a luxury buyer seeks.

Not only did Jaguar have to drive specific demand among prospects, but it had to reduce the risk of purchase significantly and become a desirable icon once again among a wider audience.

The problem was that Jaguar was a small player in the luxury automotive category. Total sales volume in 2012 was less than 5% of either BMW or Mercedes. To outpace the predicted category growth meant taking share from well-established competitors who invested hundreds of millions in marketing every year and enjoyed significant share of voice. In comparison to Audi, BMW, Mercedes-Benz and Lexus, Jaguar's share of voice for this campaign was 4% in China, 5% in Germany, 10% in the UK and 6% in the USA.

Having been ignored for years, Jaguar had to find a way to get its voice heard in this crowded landscape. This would require compelling messages over time, delivered in all the right channels, to the right people and amplified through social sharing and word-of-mouth. This would be the only way Jaguar could punch above its limited media weight.

THE MASTER PLAN

Marketing had to make it clear that it was a new generation's turn to be seduced by Jaguar. The strategy was to get people to buy into Jaguar emotionally, intellectually and financially through breakthrough content and cultural buzz. The idea was to create irresistible desire for the brand using the F-Type as an open invitation to experience a modern Jaguar. Put simply, it was "Your Turn" to experience the sex appeal and drama of a Jaguar. To create permission to buy among influencers called for the creation of a desirable image and make the "Your Turn" invitation compelling through engaging content with mass reach (Figure 2).

Figure 2. The campaign theme   Figure 3. Awakening interest

Two pieces of content were created on the theme of desire. Jaguar commissioned the song "Burning Desire" from Lana Del Rey, a hugely-popular global artist with a growing fan base and seductive style similar to Jaguar. In addition, Jaguar partnered with Ridley Scott productions and Damien Lewis, prominent British star of *Homeland*, to create a short film. Using film industry style PR this *Desire* film reached influencers in entertainment, lifestyle, and broadcast channels. Additionally, each market identified local celebrity ambassadors to create rich social content that would appeal to their own fans and grow engagement with Jaguar.

The campaign for F-Type unfolded over three phases. The communication strategy was to create "disruptive seduction" at each phase, creating emotional appeal and maximum impact for the invitation to drive.

Phase 1. Awaken desire: September-December 2012
The F-Type was revealed at the Paris Motor Show. Lana Del Rey performed the new Jaguar song which was streamed across global media channels. Trade and lifestyle press quickly amplified the impact. Intrigued prospects were encouraged to register their interest on Jaguar's digital channels (Figure 3).

To entice automotive fans, an enthusiast press campaign began to run 'spy shots' of final F-Type prototypes wrapped in campaign camouflage. As people registered, they were rewarded with an advanced online configurator and monthly "F-Type" videos such as 'Future', 'Focused', 'Fearless', and 'Fierce', each detailing a seductive aspect of the car. It had been years since Jaguar got headlines in a publication like *Hollywood Reporter*, but the release of the *Desire* film trailer created positive buzz from the entertainment industry, creating intrigue about the new image to new audiences.

Phase 2. Seduced by desire: January-April 2013
The campaign continued to create desire and drive people to Jaguar's online content. CRM began in earnest to encourage pre-registration and future test-drives, while further PR resulted in global front-page headlines. On Valentine's Day Jaguar released a music video for "Burning Desire" which received 13 million views.

In March, the full 13-minute *Desire* short film appeared, generating 200 articles and over £2 million in PR value. Interested parties could now download a stunning iPad app created with Road Inc. showcasing the F-Type with historic automotive greats.

Phase 3. Give in to desire: May-August 2013
The F-Type went on sale, and it was now officially "Your Turn" to drive it (Figure 4 a,b,c). The three main markets, Germany, UK and the US, received significant support in television, print and outdoor. In China, the primary way to reach this audience was consumer auto shows, where Jaguar showed F-Type as a modern classic.

Figures 4a, b & c. Print ads

Major social media programmes were launched to give new audiences the chance to experience Jaguar's cars for themselves. These social activities, especially those with built-in local celebrity fan bases, created valuable brand content and earned media. But most importantly they demonstrated the modern Jaguar message and placed the brand into everyday conversation.

SURPASSING EXPECTATIONS

Business results

By October of 2013, Jaguar had exceeded all sales goals. In each of the four markets sales far exceeded objectives, outpacing the average growth of its main rivals: Audi, BMW, Lexus, and Mercedes-Benz (Table 1).

Table 1

	Sales volume growth 12 months Nov-Oct			
	11-12 actual	12-13 objective	12-13 actual	Year-on-year increase
China				
Competitive set	941,208	NA	1,110,686	18%
Jaguar	8,102	50%	14,168	75%
Germany				
Competitive set	807,761	NA	783,392	-3%
Jaguar	3,193	15%	4,151	30%
UK				
Competitive set	349,035	NA	387,170	11%
Jaguar	13,721	15%	16,325	19%
US				
Competitive set	881,985	NA	1,019,374	16%
Jaguar	12,140	15%	15,160	25%

Source: Polk IHS
Competitive set: Lexus, Audi, Mercedes-Benz, BMW combined

The home market of the UK had set itself an additional goal of outselling the iconic Porsche convertibles over the spring/summer period. The F-Type, priced right between the Porsche Boxster and 911, beat all expectations, outselling 911 convertibles by 3:1 and Boxster by 20%.

BEHAVIOURAL AND ATTITUDINAL RESULTS

The objective of increasing unique visitors beat targets in each market (Table 2). Online test-drive requests met the goal of doubling for the year-on-year (YOY) period of September-August. The UK actually tripled from 2,020 to 6,381 requests, Germany doubled from 524 to 1,131, China showed an astonishing 10x increase from 205 to 2,583 and the US jumped from 2,095 to 4,926.

Table 2

	Total unique visitors – 12 months Sept-August			
	11-12 actual	13 objective	12-13 actual	YOY increase
China	6.2M	100%	13M	107%
Germany	.86M	30%	1.3M	47%
UK	4.1M	5%	4.4M	7%
US	5.4M	20%	6.8M	26%

Source: Jaguar web analytics

The clear push from content to the online experience allowed each market to achieve their individual goals of increasing online car configurations across the range by 50%, with the US up 87%, the UK 83%, Germany 230%, and China 125%.

PR and social media goals were also exceeded in all four markets.
- In China there were 3.8 million impressions, far more than the press reach ambition of three million, along with coverage on major news networks. The digital films featuring local celebrities helped to grow Jaguar's social credibility and presence.
- Germany achieved the press reach goal of three million and PR sentiment was overwhelmingly positive. This was a huge breakthrough for a British brand in the homeland of the main competition. Additionally, a dedicated social portal for F-Type events beat the target of 5,000 users by 400.
- In the UK press reach outstripped the goal of 25 million by reaching almost 30 million. On Facebook, the UK hit its highest-ever post engagement result during the main social summer push, ranking second in June and third in August on engagement for all brands in the UK.
- In the US Jaguar fulfilled its aim of one million 'likes' on Facebook by September 2013 and more than doubled the press impression target to over two billion.

All images appearing in this case study are reproduced by permission of Jaguar.

CHAPTER 8

08

Marketing sustainability

Sustainability has always been an important concept for me. As companies we have the power to make a huge difference to the environment in the broadest sense while benefitting the business at the same time, both in terms of the bottom line and employee motivation.

When I was at Procter & Gamble we did the Ariel 'Turn to 30°' campaign which not only gripped the imagination of consumers pleased that even small actions could make a difference, but it also gave us a competitive edge.

I believe we are slowly seeing a resurgence in what I call responsible marketing. And quite rightly: it should be a key part of the corporate agenda because it delivers the results, as these three cases show.

- At Unilever, the innovation in packaging technology has been an industry game-changer. Not only have consumers been won over to the new technology but the company is making huge savings in its business processes.

- The Fairtrade story highlights the power of a clear vision of sustainability to give the brand a coherent identity worldwide despite the organisation being a federation rather than a hierarchy. A carefully-plotted segmentation model and cleverly-leveraged corporate partnerships contributed to its success.

- Finally, British Gas shows how to be single-minded in tackling a big sustainability challenge – install smart meters in every house by 2020 – and create a powerful competitive advantage in an area of relatively low engagement.

Christian Woolfenden
Global Marketing Director
Paddy Power

UNILEVER SMALL CANS
Good things come in small packages

SNAPSHOT
Unilever's ground-breaking new packaging technology has not only rewritten the rules for the industry but speeded up its journey toward sustainability.

AGENCIES
Lowe Group, Clarion Communications

KEY INSIGHTS
- Ten years of research into a more sustainable way to package aerosol deodorants has resulted in a compressed can technology that is transforming the landscape for the company both economically and environmentally.
- This is the first time the company has introduced an innovation across three key brands at the same time.
- Consumers and retailers have been won over to the new technology through a high-profile marketing campaign highlighting the superior benefits of the compressed technology both in terms of its use but also for the planet.

SUMMARY
With 80% of consumers in the UK and Ireland preferring aerosol deodorants to roll-ons and stick formats, in 2013 Unilever set out to revolutionise the existing aerosol deodorant category with a compressed product. This is part of the overall Unilever mission to halve the greenhouse gas impact and waste associated with the disposal of its products by 2020 while significantly reducing consumers' environmental footprint through its ambitious Sustainable Living Plan.

The result of 10 years research and innovation, the compressed technology marks the first packaging reduction initiative for the traditional aerosol in almost 50 years. It is also the first major move by any manufacturer to make the category more sustainable. Using 50% less propellant gas than previous formats, 28% less aluminium packaging and with a 25% lower carbon footprint per can, the new product was rolled out in 2013 simultaneously across Unilever's Sure Women, Dove and Vaseline brands.

The format is half the size of the traditional aerosol deodorants but lasts just as long and is priced the same. Its sustainability credentials have shaken up the industry for the first time in almost half a century.

Supported by a £12.8 million marketing campaign to help consumers understand the new format, Unilever sold 12 million compressed cans in just 12 months and met its year-end sales target three months early. The smaller cans have also meant that more can be included per delivery, resulting in fewer lorry journeys.

By encouraging consumers to switch to the 75ml cans from the 150ml sprays, Unilever saved 339 tonnes of carbon in the year after launch, equivalent to the average emissions of a car travelling 61 times around the earth.

BREAKING NEW GROUND

The pioneering launch of Unilever's compressed range of women's deodorants in February 2013 heralded the first packaging reduction initiative for aerosol deodorants since they hit the shelves in the 1960s. It was also the first major move by any manufacturer to make the deodorant category more sustainable.

Half the size of previous cans, lasting just as long and priced the same, Unilever's Dove, Sure and Vaseline deodorants – which account for a quarter of the value of the UK retail deodorant market – shrunk from 150ml to 75ml, significantly reducing packaging, greenhouse gas emissions and waste (Figure 1).

The game-changing move means the company, which invested in a new production line to produce the format, is a step closer to achieving its Sustainable Living Plan ambition, a strategy to double the size of its business while reducing its environmental footprint and increasing its positive social impact by 2020.

The ground-breaking new product development (NPD) was rolled out as a cross-brand initiative – the first time Unilever introduced an innovation across three key brands at

Lasts as long
with less packaging

Figure 1. The new compressed packaging

the same time. Supported by a £12.8 million marketing campaign including TV, print and in-store advertising, the activity combined mass awareness and education, helping to develop consumers' understanding of the new format.

Thanks to a re-engineered spray system and reduced height, weight and diameter each compressed package includes:
- 50% less propellant gas than previous formats while still delivering the same level of deodorant active with each spray.
- 28% less aluminium packaging.
- 25% lower carbon footprint because less propellant gas and aluminium is used in the production of compressed aerosols.

By encouraging consumers to switch from dilute 150ml sprays to compressed 75ml cans, Unilever saved 339 tonnes of carbon in just 12 months since launch. This is equal to the average emissions of a car travelling 61 times around the earth. The cans not only reduce Unilever's and consumers' carbon footprints, but the use of less aluminium means Unilever avoids over- extraction of the metal. Reducing waste across the value chain is extremely important: all of Unilever's factories in the UK are rated zero non-hazardous waste to landfill and 27% of Unilever's energy now comes from renewable sources.

But the savings don't stop there:
- Less plastic in the cans means less waste to landfill and 53% more products on a pallet so that 856 boxes can now fit into one pallet compared to the previous 560.
- Taking up less space in transport means compressed cans are directly responsible for fewer lorries pumping their emissions into our atmosphere.
- The technology has also allowed Unilever to fill its trucks with cross-category products, meaning space saved by one product can be used by another.
- In the store, smaller cans take up less space on shelf, less storage space at the back of the shop and offer increased rate of sale as retailers have 15% more space on shelf.

GETTING THE MESSAGE ACROSS
While the industry-wide benefits of compressed cans were obvious, communicating and educating consumers about their advantages and changing shopper habits was another matter. As the largest step change in the category for almost half a century, success relied heavily on ensuring retailers and consumers were fully educated to the benefits of the new format.

Only something with maximum impact would do. Clarion Communications developed a trade press campaign reflecting Unilever's 100% commitment to the new format as part of the company's long- term strategy to make sustainable living commonplace and generate excitement and buzz within the industry.

The Grocer magazine, the UK's leading B2B publication for the retail trade, shrank from its usual A4 to an A5 'compressed' format complete with a special edition front cover to be distributed exclusively to 60,000 key decision makers on *The Grocer's* subscription list. The strapline 'good things do come in small packages' further drove home Unilever's investment in sustainable innovation.

The activity demonstrated a natural synergy between both the publication and the new format, communicating an important message to the industry and prompting immediate responses from industry heavy-weights.

The industry-first campaign delivered more than 120 separate pieces of media coverage. With the retail trade in no doubt about Unilever's market leading NPD, it was time to educate the consumer.

The same tactic used for the trade was applied to London's free tabloid newspaper *Metro*, targeting 300,000 commuters with a mini edition with the 'smaller size, same great content' message. The venture was accompanied by a feature examining the rise of 'green' consumers and efforts by manufacturers to produce more environmentally-friendly products and packaging.

PROMOTING BRAND BENEFITS

But simply conveying the eco-credentials of packaging across three very different brands, at a time when consumer scepticism was commonplace, was not enough. Demonstrating what each distinct brand had to offer in compressed format was crucial and brand specific campaigns vital. With the category message that compressed cans are better for the environment clear, branded communications began.

With 17% improved dryness protection versus its 150ml equivalent, Sure consumers were challenged to 'do more' both physically and environmentally. A different tactic was required for Dove, whose heritage lies in beauty and care. Instead consumers were promised 'our best care in a little can' as well as a softer, drier and less-cold product compared to other aerosols thanks to the decreased use of propellant gas.

The key message was that by compressing its deodorants Unilever was not only significantly reducing the environmental impact of its products, but it was putting consumers first by offering them a far superior proposition, with benefits over and above their conventional predecessors.

There were no compromises to be made in terms of product quality or price premium, enabling the consumer to reduce their own environmental footprint with no trade-off on performance or price.

Working alongside efficiency experts WRAP, the Aluminium Packaging Recycling Organisation (ALUPRO) and the British Aerosol Manufacturers' Association (BAMA), Unilever has encouraged local authorities to accept consumers' empty aerosol cans in kerbside collections and recycling banks. As a result, 86% of local authorities now collect aerosols for recycling, an increase from 63%. It means that nearly six million households are able to recycle aerosols.

In addition, Unilever has actively encouraged consumers to recycle those cans with a raft of marketing campaigns, including a high-profile collaboration with Sainsbury's encouraging shoppers to recycle their bathroom packaging on the supermarket's Bag for Life.

SPEARHEADING SUSTAINABILITY

The result of a decade of research and leading-edge innovation, Unilever's compressed aerosol cans are enabling the company to make vital progress in achieving its ambitious Sustainable Living Plan.

The 10-year plan is aimed at doubling the size of the business while halving its impact on the environment and it has three main goals:
• To improve the health and well-being of one billion people.
• To reduce the environmental impact associated with the making and use of products.
• To source 100% of all agricultural raw materials sustainably.

A key goal underpinning the strategy is making products more sustainable, including:
• Halving the greenhouse gas impact of products across the lifecycle by 2020.
• Halving the waste associated with the disposal of products by 2020.

To put this into perspective, if one million consumers switched to compressed deodorants and bought five cans a year each, Unilever could help the planet save:

- 720 tonnes of CO_2 per year, or the equivalent amount of emissions from a car travelling 130 times round the earth or consumed by 32,700 trees, which would cover the area occupied by 23 football pitches.
- Enough aluminium to make 25,600 bikes or three million cola cans.

RECORD RESULTS

In just 12 months since launch Unilever had successfully persuaded consumers to make the switch tenfold. In that time more than 12 million cans of compressed female deodorants had been sold across the Sure Women, Dove and Vaseline brands, with Unilever's conversion into compressed year-end target met in September 2013.

Customer satisfaction research showed that more than 70% of consumers prefer the look and feel of the new compressed cans, while the format was also given a rating of 4.6 out of 5, with 94% of consumers giving the product at least four stars.

Figure 2. The male compressed range

The new format has also won a host of awards including:
- *The Grocer* Product of the Year 2013.
- Best Packaging of the Year Award – Beauty Awards 2013.
- Waitrose Treading Lightly Award.
- Aerosol of the Year Award 2013 – British Aerosol Manufacturing Awards.
- Special Innovation Award – Pure Beauty Awards 2013.

The company is now in the midst of compressing its entire female portfolio by reducing its 250ml ranges to 125ml. The sustainable format has also introduced simultaneously across Sure Men, Dove Men +Care, Lynx and Vaseline Men brands, backed by a £15 million marketing spend including TV advertising (Figure 2). Research has revealed that men are receptive to the change. As a result Unilever's compressed format was set to account for 42% of the company's deodorant portfolio by the end of 2014.

All images appearing in this case study are reproduced by permission of Unilever.

THE FAIRTRADE FOUNDATION
Finding the perfect brand balance

SNAPSHOT

The Fairtrade Foundation's far-reaching marketing strategy gave the brand renewed impetus without alienating its grassroots campaigners.

KEY INSIGHTS

- The Fairtrade Foundation created a marketing function in a bid to re-energise its brand and broaden its global reach among consumers and business partners while staying true to its core principles.
- The subsequent brand revamp and campaigns, both offline and online, were developed alongside in-depth consumer research to produce actionable segmentation.
- The result was a step-change in brand awareness, familiarity and value among consumers and businesses, a consolidation of its trusted position and a re-engagement with its grassroots movement.

SUMMARY

The fair trade movement in the UK goes back more than 20 years. Its roots lie with a group of concerned citizens who wanted to form fairer trading links to give a better deal to those at the end of the international supply chains. These pioneering consumers and businesses created a social movement which raised awareness of unfair trade and helped create a market for ethical products.

In the first decade, the emergence of a single Fairtrade mark and the energy of the social movement together led to a force with huge potential to transform the trade landscape. However, by 2007, less than £500 million worth of Fairtrade goods were sold in the UK. So, in 2007 the Fairtrade Foundation brought in a marketing function to reposition the Fairtrade brand for the public and develop a compelling proposition for businesses to join the movement and help grow it.

The results were definitive. With a limited budget, Fairtrade globalised the brand, found an accessible tone of voice, made its understanding of the ethical consumer more sophisticated, took its communities online, refocused its campaigners and translated all this into a successful commercial proposition.

A CHANGING CONTEXT
The Fairtrade Foundation was founded in 1988 in response to the growing grassroots movement in civil society that demanded that products should be sourced from developing countries on terms that would empower impoverished farmers to work their own way out of poverty.

With a mark to show ethically-minded consumers that the products guaranteed a fairer deal for farmers, the Fairtrade movement created a mental shortcut, or brand, which became the gold standard in a burgeoning ethical sector. It also united the separate country movements under one mark so Fairtrade could go global as a labelling option for multinational companies (Figure 1).

1994 – 2002   2002 – 2008

2008 – 2010   2011 onwards

Figure 1. Emergence of an international brand

Awareness, familiarity and sales grew steadily, thanks to campaigners. As supply chains became more established, availability of products and traded volumes began

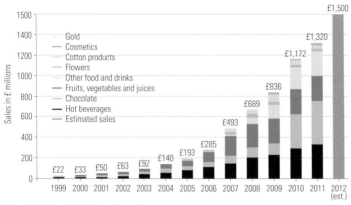

Figure 2. Sales of UK Fairtrade products

to hit critical mass. The support of key retailers such as the Co-operative and Sainsbury's made core Fairtrade products like coffee and bananas available (Figure 2).

By 2008/9 the sales outlook was positive, but signs were that future growth was not going to be easy. The UK was in recession, businesses were cutting costs and consumer concerns were increasingly close to home. Fairtrade was no longer alone in the market. A new marketing strategy was needed if Fairtrade was to scale up volume and go mainstream.

TAKING THE BRAND GLOBAL

Globalising the Fairtrade brand was an appropriate starting point for expanding the brand and approaching mainstream markets for a number of reasons:

- Global brands looking to build purpose into their brands wanted a globally-consistent certifier, so marketing campaigns could be replicated across borders.
- Because of cash limitations in each Fairtrade market, investing in quality brand development was only feasible with combined budgets.
- Financial constraints meant that 'stealing with pride' was imperative for smaller markets to access good marketing assets from larger markets. So messaging, design and imagery needed to be consistent.

The Foundation moved quickly and successfully from an inconsistent base to a global brand within 12 months, despite notable obstacles not typically found in the private sector, such as:

- The lack of a 'head office' to direct content and implementation. Fairtrade International in Bonn has a central co-ordinating role, but the international network

operates as a federation rather than a hierarchy. With separate founding members, boards and budgets in each market, participation in a project like this and compliance was entirely voluntary.
- The politics of Fairtrade are different in different countries, with variances culturally specific and often emotive. Messaging in Austria, for example, had focused on child labour while in South Africa black empowerment was a priority. In France, Fairtrade is positioned as a real alternative to conventional trade, not as a partner of multinationals. The Swiss, on the other hand, position Fairtrade as a corporate solution.
- Awareness of Fairtrade in different markets varies greatly, from single digit awareness in markets such as Poland and South Korea to 90% in the UK. This called for more basic communication of what Fairtrade is in some markets, with a greater need for emotional connection in others.

The guidelines managed to walk the line between global consistency and appropriate flexibility in implementation, based on the shared vision (see 'A shared vision'). They were adopted fully in all markets, from the most established like the UK to the least like South Korea (Figures 3 and 4).

Figure 3. New international brand identity

Figure 4. New international brand

STRIKING THE RIGHT NOTE IN THE UK

A stronger, consistent look and feel helped establish a strong visual identity globally for Fairtrade and met the need of global licensees to roll out partner marketing activity internationally. Nonetheless, a marketing campaign would be needed which would address the particular needs of the UK market in order to:

• Deepen engagement.
• Encourage people to move from being positive about Fairtrade to more active purchasing, more often.
• Develop a campaigning voice and style flexible enough to galvanise supporters while convincing mainstream brands that Fairtrade could fit with their brand positioning.

The result was a creative strategy to make it stand out from increasingly generic development communication and appeal to less committed, positively pre-disposed shoppers. The first campaign, The Big Swap for Fairtrade Fortnight 2010 (Figure 5), was based on a strong promotional template which delivered a significant level of partner activity.

Figure 5. The Big Swap for Fairtrade Fortnight 2010

• Enough advertisers came together under the Big Swap banner to sponsor a 'Fairtrade Big Swap' ad break on Channel 4.
• Over one million 'Swaps' to Fairtrade were registered online by supporters and shoppers.
• Mainstream brands had just begun switching and Starbucks turned its stores over to a blanket Fairtrade message with a Big Swap sales promotion.
• In addition, Cadbury TV advertised a brand promotion swapping wrappers for music.

Awareness of Fairtrade Fortnight grew from 30% in 2009 to 49% in 2010. Moreover, 25% of people claimed to have bought a product as a result of seeing or hearing about Fairtrade during the Fairtrade Fortnight period.

REVEALING UNDERLYING CONSUMER TRUTHS

The next stage was to understand the target audience better in order to go mainstream and help partners. That meant moving from an understanding based on 'gut feel' to a more sophisticated segmentation. To do that, 2,000 consumers were studied to identify their characteristics in relation to attitudes and behaviours (Figure 6).

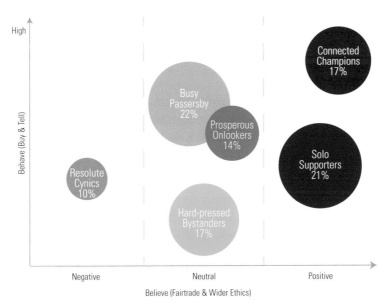

Figure 6. Consumer characteristics

The results revealed that:
- 10% were 'resolute cynics'.
- 22% were 'busy passersby'.
- 14% were 'prosperous onlookers'.
- 17% were 'hard-pressed bystanders'.
- 21% were 'solo supporters'.
- 17% were 'connected champions'.

This showed that the best opportunity for creating greater commitment to Fairtrade lay in two key audiences representing some 40% of the population.

• Solo supporters were an older group of ethical shoppers with strong convictions and set ideas, which favoured Fairtrade. They were well-off and tended to over-index in terms of Fairtrade spend. They were less likely to act for Fairtrade or spread the word generally.

• Connected champions were a younger group of people. Socially-networked online and offline, they were environmentally and socially aware and connected with other people expansively on their views and perspectives.

Fairtrade thus decided to rebalance its marketing and press activity to ensure efforts were reaching across the spectrum, but with a greater emphasis on connected champions as an opportunity to expand the campaigning nature to a broader constituency than the traditional Fairtrade campaigner. Given budgets, it was also pragmatic to target and ignite an active online audience. These consumers were responsive to simple but meaningful communication on the need for Fairtrade and the impact of their purchases.

SOCIAL MEDIA IMMERSION

In 2009 Fairtrade's social media presence was just starting to grow. With the launch of Fairtrade cosmetics that year, the Foundation decided to increase the digital base. Time and budget were invested in campaigns about new and lesser-known product categories which would make positively-predisposed consumers re-evaluate Fairtrade, engage and share.

Figure 7. 'Make beauty fair' campaign

To communicate at a brand level a range of digital mechanics was created which made it easier for consumers to engage. Figure 7 shows the 'Make beauty fair' campaign, while other campaigns centred around buying South African wine, labelling and chocolate. While succeeding in growing Fairtrade's digital engagement, these campaigns also integrated with licensee communications, helping them give purpose to their brands.

The result was a transformation in digital interaction between the Foundation and its supporters. Between 2009 and 2012 digital metrics grew exponentially. For example, while during 2009 some 70,000 people viewed a piece of digital content from Fairtrade, in 2012 that figure was almost 1,000,000. With overall annual budget growth no greater than 10% per annum, this was a tremendous indication of how mainstream the direct engagement had become.

A significant secondary benefit was that the commercial licensees now considered the supporter engagement channels as a valuable route to market for their brand and corporate social responsibility (CSR) communications, and a mechanism that could deliver value for money for their license fee.

This has also encouraged increasingly innovative ideas to encourage deeper engagement with Fairtrade. For example, in February 2013 the Ask Malawi project allowed consumers to connect directly with a community in Malawi to better understand them, their challenges and the impact of Fairtrade.

REINVIGORATING THE NETWORKS

The campaigns network is the backbone of the Fairtrade movement, with 32% of people learning about Fairtrade through family, friends and colleagues, while 16% hear about it through education, community and faith groups. Word-of-mouth is a key asset. Brand partners highly value the networks and Fairtrade's privileged access to them.

The risk in mainstreaming is that it leaves many campaigners feeling the job is done and they no longer campaign with the passion they had when Fairtrade was young. To address this, from 2009 the strategy was updated to:
- Improve the tools campaigners had to reach mainstream consumers, bringing them closer to delivering the strategy and involving them in the process of mainstreaming.
- Invest in those campaigning groups where the energy lay such as schools, where there is most interest in new groups reaching Fairtrade status.

• Link Fairtrade to related issues: highlighting its impact as an environmental standard, developing mining standards, linking the plight of developing world farmers to domestic farmers and showing how poor countries are bearing the brunt of global environmental deterioration.

BUILDING BRANDS WITH PURPOSE

Fairtrade lives or dies by its ability to convert everything it does into a compelling business case for brands. Companies have needed to be convinced that Fairtrade is the best way that they can build purpose into their brands. The success of the marketing of Fairtrade thus has had a strong business-to-business dimension. Key aspects of the marketing strategy have included:

• A value and research-based business case, outlining the financial and brand equity potential of a switch to Fairtrade.

• Sector-specific e-communications, delivering messages on the impact of Fairtrade on supply chains and farmers, and product availability.

• An annual conference with appropriate thought leaders, producers and new brands to engage current and prospective licensees in the Fairtrade story.

• Using the Foundation's understanding of connected champions and solo supporters for prospective partner brands to suggest marketing strategies.

FAST FACTS

• Farmers and workers in 59 countries sell Fairtrade-certified products in the UK.

• 75% of all Fairtrade producers are small-scale farmers.

• 668 groups of farmers and workers supply Fairtrade products to the UK.

Figure 8. New brands becoming certified

DOING WELL BY DOING GOOD

All these efforts were paying off in a number of ways:

- The delivery of new brands to Fairtrade certification (Figure 8).
- Fairtrade sales growth.
- Growth in awareness, familiarity, trust and active choice (Figure 9).
- Continued growth in the grass roots movements as the brand has become more mainstream.
- Delivery of value to farmers (Figure 10).

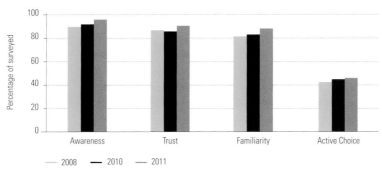

Figure 9. Growth in awareness, familiarity, trust and active choice

Figure 10. Delivery of value to farmers

All images appearing in this case study are reproduced by permission of the Fairtrade Foundation.

BRITISH GAS
Smart marketing pays off

SNAPSHOT

British Gas transformed its customers' understanding and usage of smart energy meters through a multi-channel campaign that saw installation reach the one-million milestone.

AGENCIES

CHI & Partners, Carat

KEY INSIGHTS

- With all energy companies having to install smart meters in customers' homes by 2020, British Gas took a pro-active approach with a clever integrated strategy to boost both awareness and ultimately take-up of the technology.
- The use of multiple formats, including an energetic social media campaign, broke through what had been widespread ignorance of the benefits of smart metering.
- By the end of 2013 not only had the company installed a million smart meters but customers were actively seeking to lower energy usage thanks to the company's information and support.

SUMMARY

British Gas is the UK's largest energy supplier, serving around 12 million homes in Britain. While all energy companies are required to fit smart meters in their customers' homes by 2020, in early 2013 there was still a lot of confusion among consumers about what they do. This was having a negative impact on take-up of the meters, so British Gas devised and ran a through-the-line marketing programme in the second half of 2013 to increase awareness and understanding, along with persuading more customers to accept them.

The resulting multi-channel marketing approach shifted awareness and understanding of smart meters by both British Gas customers and customers of other suppliers by seven percentage points. It also changed the way the company engaged with its customers by helping them manage their energy consumption on a much more precise basis.

By the end of 2013 the company had reached the one million installation milestone, with more meters installed than any other supplier. Even more significantly, a survey of customers in October 2013 found that 79% of those using both smart meters and in-home display were more aware of their consumption, with nine out of 10 taking steps to reduce usage.

TACKLING LOW LEVELS OF AWARENESS
Smart meters are reckoned to be the most significant energy innovation in recent history. The Department of Energy and Climate Change (DECC) aims for smart meters to be installed as standard by 2020. Not only do smart meters help save energy and money by giving customers more control over usage, they also send meter readings automatically, putting an end to estimated bills.

British Gas is committed to rolling out smart meters to its customers. However, at the beginning of 2013 it could see that smart meters were still barely understood. Only 49% of bill payers said they had heard of them while a mere 5% claimed to have one.

These figures reflected acute confusion about them, as the company found:
• Only 38% understood what a smart meter was and how it worked.
• The same number believed it was a monitor to show how much energy your appliance is using.
• Just 11% knew it was a monitor plugged into the mains to show energy consumption.
• 15% had no idea what they were.

DECC research showed that there was a clear link between those with a greater knowledge of smart meters and an interest in having one installed. British Gas thus faced a three-pronged challenge:
• Increase awareness of smart meters.
• Drive greater understanding and engagement.
• Help customers manage their energy consumption through installation of smart meters.

A MULTI-CHANNEL MISSION

The starting point was the launch of a multi-channel campaign in July 2013. This was a long-term fully integrated campaign to ensure maximum awareness of smart meters and their benefits. Above-the-line advertising was used to boost awareness of the push to roll-out the meters on a much greater scale – the first-ever TV ad to do so. It was placed during key programmes and at popular viewing times.

Other media included radio, press, digital, direct, PR and social media, with customers encouraged to register their interest in smart meters. High-profile formats such as digital out-of-home, press cover wraps and interactive/educational digital sites helped get the message across more broadly (Figures 1 and 2). Taken in total, it led to 60% of customers saying they wanted to find out more, which was 20% above the average. This was supported by targeted social media activity to engage consumers even more directly.

Figure 1. *Metro* cover wrap

Figure 2. The screen at Canary Wharf

- For example, a dedicated partnership hub encouraging people to explore the benefits of smart meters attracted 22,000 unique hub visits, 9,000 competition entries, 350 thread interactions and positive sentiment measured at more than 75%.
- A dedicated '90-day energy plan' hub explaining the value of meters had 13,000 page views, interactions with 1,700 mothers and a seven-minute dwell time on the energy plan thread.
- An important element of the campaign was the use of a combination of professional and consumer bloggers.

Direct marketing was geared to encouraging take-up. Having consulted a behavioural scientist, Dr Robert Metcalfe, the test and learn direct marketing campaigns achieved an average response rate of 21%, while the segmented versions saw a 30% conversion rate. The email invitation for a smart meter, including a video demo, had a click-through rate 46% higher than average.

Seven videos were also created for 'frequently-asked questions' featuring a 'smart energy' expert. Launched on YouTube, they had over 120,000 combined views (Figures 3, 4 and 5). To keep customers engaged and ensure access, emails were sent to customers ahead of the installation.

Finally, British Gas developed the Smart Energy Report which was sent to customers with meters on a regular basis, either by email or post (Figure 6). It gave them a breakdown of their energy usage by lighting, heating, cooking, appliances and hot water. It also drilled down to historic usage, comparing it to other households, as well as providing personalised tips. Of those customers interviewed, 80% said they read it and more than three-quarters said it was useful. The average dwell time on the report on the website was 17 minutes.

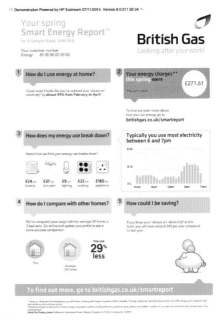

Figure 3, 4 and 5. FAQ video   Figure 6. Smart Energy Report

SIGNS OF SUCCESS

By the end of 2013 actual awareness had increased by 7% (Figure 7). The campaign had also met its objective of strengthening customer engagement, while there was a pronounced rise in customers' understanding of their usage. By creating personalised reports based on half-hourly readings of customers' energy consumption, they could see what they were using with each appliance and could be offered personalised tips on saving.

By the end of 2013 actual awareness increased by 7%

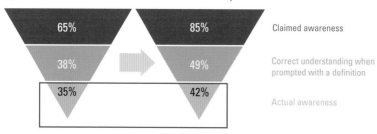

Figure 7. Awareness of smart meters
Source: YouGov omnibus Q1 2013/A&C tracker Oct/Nov 2013

Explaining the benefits of these half-hourly reads and subsequent reports led to an opt-in to these half-hourly reads of 84%. Other figures were equally impressive.

- There was a 375% increase in registrations of interest at britishgas.co.uk/smart.
- Over 120,000 combined views of YouTube installation videos.
- A significant 87% of smart customers said that the Smart Energy Report was informative.
- More than two-thirds felt that the report helped them manage their usage.
- Almost 80% of those using the in-home display were more aware of their consumption.
- Nine out of 10 people were taking simple steps to reduce usage.
- 40% of them had tackled wider issues within the home.
- Just under 55% had saved money, with over two-thirds identifying savings of up to £75.

By December 2013 there were over a million British Gas smart meters in Britain's homes and businesses, with one being installed by the company every two minutes.

All images appearing in this case study are reproduced by permission of British Gas.

CHAPTER 9

09

Marketing to make a difference

Companies and brands are under scrutiny as never before. As the clamour grows for businesses to be a force for good as well as meeting their financial obligations, they are under pressure to put in place marketing programmes that can offer demonstrable benefits beyond the bottom line.

These three case studies are great examples of just what can be achieved. Sainsbury's partnered with Channel 4 to develop a ground-breaking campaign with both short- and long-term objectives: in the short-term, make the Paralympics 2012 as high-profile as the Olympic Games had been, and, longer-term, transform attitudes to disability generally. Both the Sainsbury's and Channel 4 brands benefitted hugely from a carefully-crafted, meticulously-planned campaign in terms of customer relationships and employee engagement as well as business performance.

Paddy Power's cheeky attitude to marketing worked perfectly in helping tackle the tricky issue of homophobia in football with its first corporate social responsibility campaign. By forming an alliance with Stonewall and using the simple device of sending out rainbow-coloured bootlaces to every professional football club, the company generated headlines for the cause far beyond the money spent to launch it.

Depaul is a tiny charity that thought big to boost donations for its efforts to help young homeless people find a place to stay. Well aware that donor fatigue was becoming a major issue, it thought laterally and imaginatively to find a solution. Setting up a commercial offshoot that sells boxes to people moving house is a striking example of how business really can make a difference.

Craig Inglis
Director, Marketing
John Lewis

SAINSBURY'S AND CHANNEL 4

Marketing game-changer

SNAPSHOT
The marketing dream team of Sainsbury's and Channel 4 ensured that the Paralympics was no longer seen as the poor relation of the Olympics Games but an outstanding event in its own right.

AGENCY
AMVBBDO

KEY INSIGHTS
- The decision by Sainsbury's and Channel 4 to work together to make the Paralympics as high-profile as the Olympics was one of the biggest marketing challenges either had ever undertaken.
- It led to a carefully-crafted, multi-platform strategy that saw Sainsbury's developing projects to engage staff and customers aligned with Channel 4's imaginative broadcasting approach to maximise audience appeal.
- The results not only made sponsorship and broadcasting history, but transformed attitudes toward disability.

SUMMARY
Sainsbury's and Channel 4 took a leap of faith when they decided to collaborate on a large-scale sponsorship of the London 2012 Paralympics since neither had been involved in the Games before.

The retailer based its contribution on 'Here's to extraordinary' to set the right tone, and launched a range of initiatives to get the excitement mounting. For example, it turned its staff into advocates by giving every employee the opportunity to try a Paralympic sport, encouraging them to be Games Makers and sending 5,000 members of staff to the Games themselves. It also oversaw a range of schemes and projects targeted at both schools and consumers, while the Paralympic Torch visited 550 supermarkets.

Channel 4 provided the most comprehensive Paralympics coverage ever, with more than 150 hours of television programming and a series of compelling ads. It also created content and tools to help viewers understand better the complexities of the Games.

Almost 40 million people, more than two-thirds of the UK population, watched the Games, while Sainsbury's enjoyed the highest association of any Paralympic sponsor.

GIVING THE GAMES A MARKETING MAKEOVER
Like many successes, the Paralympics held in London in 2012 looks effortless in retrospect. It was anything but. It was in large part due to two brands deciding to do something unconventional: to sponsor something marginal but important and use marketing to make Britain care about it.

Sainsbury's and Channel 4 were in an interesting position. They were the only brands in history ever to have a significant stake in the Paralympics without any involvement in the Olympics preceding it. In order for this to be a success, the partners needed to achieve three tough objectives:
• Make the Paralympics popular. To get full value, they needed to make Britain fall in love with the event. But awareness and interest in the Paralympics were low.
• Introduce a nation to new sports and new sports stars. The Olympics showed that personalities were vital to create interest. They needed to build understanding and personal connection. But they were starting from a very low base.
• To get Britain to see the athletic achievement, not the disability. Sports sponsorships tend to be more valuable that cause-related initiatives. So, if the Paralympics was seen as 'do-goodery', it would have lower value for the brands.

In addition, Sainsbury's needed to generate revenue and Channel 4 fulfil its public service remit by inspiring change in people's lives and audience growth.

This was a daunting marketing challenge (See: 'A long way to go'). The Paralympics is a hostage to the fortunes of the world's biggest sporting event. If the main Olympic

Games succeed, the Paralympics can be seen merely as a bad hangover. If they flop, few will be interested in the Paralympics. What would make all the difference is how the Games were marketed.

A LONG WAY TO GO

The results of in-depth research showed just what the partners had to overcome:
- Spontaneous awareness stood at only 16%.
- 48% of respondents were ambivalent or actively uninterested.
- Over 80% could not name a single British Paralympian.
- Half felt that disabled people could not achieve what able-bodied people could.
- 40% felt that disability would hold people back.

SAINSBURY'S STRATEGIC PILLARS

Setting the tone was crucial. Knowing that the public didn't have the language to express feelings about disability or Paralympic sport, the word 'extraordinary' was chosen to point the way to think about the difference in this context: positively, but without being patronising. This was set in the context of three distinct strategic pillars:
- Turn Sainsbury's colleagues into advocates.
- Engage Sainsbury's communities through schools.
- Engage customers in and out of stores.

1. Turn Sainsbury's colleagues into advocates

Sainsbury's saw its greatest asset as its store colleagues, which proved to be a winning decision as they became the country's biggest Paralympic fanbase. The company paired 70 local Paralympians with stores across the country, while every colleague was also given the opportunity to try a Paralympic sport. In addition, 30 colleagues were seconded to the London Organising Committee of the Olympics and Paralympic Games (LOCOG) and 45 were nominated to take part in the Paralympic Torch Relay. Finally, 150 colleagues became Games Makers and on one day 5,000 colleagues attended the Paralympics as spectators.

2. Engage Sainsbury's communities through schools

Sainsbury's has run the Active Kids scheme in schools since 2005. This proved to be a great asset. Research suggested kids had less prejudice about Paralympic sport and could create enthusiasm in households. The Million Kids Challenge provided equipment and training to schools for one million children to try a Paralympic sport. It was so popular that over 2.4 million children from 8,000 schools actually ended up getting involved, which was featured on Channel 4 news.

3. Engage customers in and out of stores

Customers were targeted with specific Paralympic activation and communication:

- Sainsbury's Super Saturday was televised on Channel 4. It included top pop acts, combined with Paralympians playing sport and opportunities for kids to have a go (Figure 1).
- The Paralympic Torch visited 550 Sainsbury's supermarkets, while 100 customers got the chance to take part in the Torch Relay.
- 12,000 tickets were given to customers.
- A communication campaign cemented the excitement among the public.

Figure 1. Sainsbury's Super Saturday

CHANNEL 4 GOES THE EXTRA MILE

As a public service broadcaster, Channel 4 has a long history of programming featuring disabled people. So, rather than simply televise the event, the channel created content and tools to help viewers better understand the Games, with programming that would help people talk and think differently about disability.

It was the biggest marketing campaign in Channel 4's history. It set itself a series of challenging goals, which involved rolling out a programme of internal change and development to start shifting perceptions:

• Commit to disabled talent on screen.
• Make Paralympics sport simple to enjoy.
• Create the best Paralympics coverage ever.

1. Commit to new disabled talent on screen.
The Paralympic Games represented an opportunity for Channel 4 to discover a new generation of disabled presenters. It conducted a talent search and rigorous training programme to ensure that at least half of the on-air team was disabled. An ex-Royal Marine, a carpenter and a former Paralympic swimmer were among the new disabled presenters uncovered by Channel 4 in the biggest talent search of its kind (Figure 2).

Figure 2. Channel 4 presenters

2. Make Paralympic sport simple to enjoy.
Research showed that a third of UK adults found the disability classifications confusing. They would be more interested in watching Paralympics sports if they had a better understanding of eligibility rules for each event. Channel 4 worked with Paralympic gold medallist Giles Long to develop LEXI, a new graphics-based system that helps viewers understand the classification used to distinguish different levels and forms of disability among Paralympic athletes.

3. Create the best Paralympics coverage (and the best ads) ever.
Channel 4 committed in its bid to LOCOG to provide the most comprehensive Paralympics coverage ever, with more than 150 hours of television programming.

This was well exceeded. Not only did afternoon coverage shift from More4 to Channel 4, but there was an additional 350 hours of live coverage online. Viewers could also keep up via Paralympics apps for mobile and tablet devices. All this was presented in association with Sainsbury's and BT.

The 'Meet the Superhumans' TV ad mixed bold close-up imagery of disabled bodies in training, competition and at rest with scenes that conjured up the extraordinary back stories of the athletes (Figure 3). This was supported by a cheeky 'Thanks for the warm-up' poster campaign around the end of the Olympics, making it quite clear that the Paralympics should be seen as a thrilling event in its own right (Figure 4).

Figure 3. 'Meet the Superhumans' TV ad

Figure 4. Poster campaign

SETTING NEW RECORDS

Both Sainsbury's and Channel 4 achieved their initial joint objectives:

- Make the Paralympics popular. Almost 40 million people tuned in, with awareness of Paralympic Games rising from 16% in 2010 to 77% by the end of September 2012.
- Introduce a nation to new sports and new sports stars. In the same period the number of people who could name a British Paralympian leapt from 18% to 41%.
- To get Britain to see the athletic achievement, not the disability. By the end of September 2012 compared to 2010, 69% vs 60% of people agreed that 'Disability does not hold you back'. In addition, 59% vs 50% agreed that 'Disabled people can achieve what able-bodied people can'.

Sainsbury's scores on all counts

Sainsbury's had the highest association of any Paralympic sponsor and the highest growth in association during the event. Such strong association naturally had a knock-on effect on brand perceptions.

- The score for brand empathy hit record levels since the start of HPI's tracking and for the first time Sainsbury's was top of the big four supermarkets.
- 'Brand awareness' and 'consideration' also hit their highest level yet.
- This positivity towards the brand was felt just as deeply among the galvanised fanbase of colleagues, with their enthusiasm for the sponsorship reaching 89%.

The magnitude of Sainsbury's success is perhaps best shown in the awareness data collected by Nielsen, the official data and research supplier to LOCOG, at the close of the Paralympics. The retailer finished 2012 as the third-most recalled Olympic sponsor, ahead of all other domestic sponsors and ahead of 16 other brands which had sponsored the Olympics and Paralympics. In other words, a brand that had sponsored only half the event, and, for the first time ever, had claimed a top three spot.

In addition, as a sponsor, Sainsbury's saw its investment rewarded, with +5.6% sales growth in the 12 weeks to September 2012 and a positive overall sponsorship return on investment and an advertising profit ROI for above-the-line at 1:4.3.

Channel 4 breaks the mould

Channel 4's coverage was pivotal.

- 56% of all viewers felt more comfortable talking about disability as a result of Channel 4's coverage.
- 83% of viewers surveyed agreed that Channel 4's coverage would improve society's perceptions of disabled people.

- 64% of viewers felt more positive towards disabled people as a result of watching Channel 4's coverage.
- 74% of viewers 12-16 felt more comfortable talking about disability as a result of Channel 4's coverage.

As a public service broadcaster, Channel 4 was not primarily seeking to profit from the event. Success was instead to be based on audience engagement.

- 11.6 million watched the Opening Ceremony (the channel's highest viewing since Big Brother 2002).
- Almost 40 million people – more than two-thirds of the UK population – watched the Paralympic Games on TV.
- By the end of the first full day, more people had watched the 2012 Paralympics on Channel 4 than viewed the whole of the Paralympics in 2008.
- During the Paralympics Games, Channel 4 was up 65% for volume and 76% for share against the same period last year.
- Three quarters (76%) agreed 'Channel 4 did a great job covering the Paralympics' (this despite some initial criticism for carrying ads).
- 36% of Paralympic viewers felt more positive towards Channel 4 overall – this measure is a particularly important determinant of success for a public service broadcaster.
- The success of the coverage is shown by Channel 4's success in winning coverage of the Sochi 2014 Winter Games and 2016 Rio Paralympic Games.

All images appearing in this case study are reproduced by permission of Sainsbury's and Channel 4.

PADDY POWER
Moving the goalposts

SNAPSHOT
A bold and highly-effective marketing campaign from betting specialists Paddy Power continued the brand's determination to grab the headlines while tackling one of the most difficult issues in sport.

AGENCIES
Crispin Porter + Bogusky, M2M, Lucky Generals

KEY INSIGHTS
- This campaign was another example of Paddy Power's strategy to transform the brand's visibility in a cut-throat and competitive market with a series of mischievous ads based on what's making news.
- On this occasion Paddy Power joined forces with Stonewall to tackle the thorny issue of homophobia in football in its first-ever corporate social responsibility (CSR) campaign — one that would be fun enough to grab attention but have a serious message as well.
- The idea — sending out rainbow-coloured bootlaces to every professional football club to wear in their next match — generated attention far beyond the tiny budget used to launch it.
- Social engagement levels soared and support for the campaign spread well beyond football, while still reflecting the brand values of both partners.

SUMMARY
Paddy Power is an international, multi-channel betting and gaming group, operating across a range of businesses and territories. It is one of the largest bookmakers (in revenue terms) in the British and Irish market and in Australia; while it launched

Paddy Power in Europe's biggest betting market, Italy, in May 2012.

Its business strategy is based on identifying large, attractive, regulated markets; investing heavily in people, product, value and brand; and leveraging its strengths in areas such as mobile and social media to deliver strong market positions.

In 2013 Paddy Power invited Stonewall, the highly-successful campaigning and lobbying organisation, to help tackle one of the toughest challenges in sport: homophobia in football. The game had at best remained silent on this issue for years, with hostility more the norm. The media had little interest in the subject, while, of 5,000 professional players, not one would speak out, let alone come out.

In just one week in September this all changed thanks to a daring and innovative campaign put together by the two organisations which involved sending rainbow bootlaces to every professional football player in Britain, and asking them to wear them, to show that they were "Right Behind Gay Footballers". A barrage of advertising, PR, digital and social media followed to marshal wider public support.

The result was truly a game-changer, garnering significant support, awareness and approval. It was delivered for less than £150,000, which was less than 1% of Paddy Power's annual budget and less than 0.2% of category spend.

This was all part of a much broader and sophisticated guerrilla marketing strategy which Paddy Power embarked on in 2012 to stand out against the big brands in the market. At the same time, it wanted to show that it put its customers at the heart of everything it does.

THE SOCIAL CHALLENGE: THE GREAT FOOTBALL TABOO

The social challenge: the great football taboo of homophobia in football is often referred to as sport's last great taboo. For instance, in 2005 the BBC asked all 20 Premier League managers for their views on the subject, but every single one declined to answer. Likewise, in 2010, the Football Association asked players to take part in an anti-homophobia video, but not one would.

At worst, there has been active hostility. World-famous managers have publicly stated their disdain for gay footballers, several players have been criticised for homophobic remarks and the tabloids have often been guilty of using similar language.

As a result of this culture, by the beginning of 2013 not a single one of Britain's 5,000 professional footballers was openly gay (and indeed the only high-profile player who had come out in the past had tragically taken his own life).

Paddy Power calculated the odds of this as over a quadragintillion to one (that's one, followed by 123 zeroes). But instead of taking bets on the subject, the company decided to do something positive by mounting its first-ever brand-led CSR campaign. After all, it prided itself on being the 'punters' champion', symbolised by the mantra: "We hear you". And, in this case, the public's views were already well ahead of the authorities': research showed that 49% of British adults agreed that "homophobia in football needs to be addressed", with only 9% disagreeing.

STANDING OUT FROM THE CROWD: AN AUDACIOUS NEW MARKETING STRATEGY

The 'Right Behind Gay Footballers' campaign was part of a broader strategy that began in 2012, setting the brand out to be on the side of the punter while being more relevant and distinct by moving from being a gambling brand to a participant in sports culture.

For example, in late 2012, at the Ryder Cup, Paddy Power developed what it called the world's first 'sky tweet'. Using five stunt planes flying at 10,000 feet above the golf course the brand invited Twitter followers to tweet real-time support for the European team.

By the end of that year the brand had achieved 50% growth in new customers and a 29% increase in net revenues. And the company is gleefully continuing this approach, sailing quite close to the wind at times. For instance, in March 2014 an ad that offered a 'money back if he walks' guarantee for betting on the Oscar Pistorius murder trial was banned by the Advertising Standards Authority.

THE COMMUNICATIONS CHALLENGE: FIGHTING THE FOOTBALL BUREAUCRACY

Paddy Power knew it wasn't the first to tackle this thorny issue. Various organisations had tried to make a difference over the years. However, they had had little success. This was partly because these attempts had been rather worthy affairs, devoid of any creativity. As one observer was quoted in *Pink News*: "However commendable, these initiatives are mostly below the radar. They make very little dent on the public consciousness and are not directly reaching most players and fans. The average person in the street is unaware they exist."

But, on top of this, previous campaigns had also fallen victim to football's bureaucracy. With so many parties involved, each with a slightly different remit and agenda, it was difficult to reach a consensus and get anything done. In England alone, interested parties included The Football Association, The Professional Footballers' Association, The Premier League, The Championship, The League Managers Association, clubs, agents, sponsors, fan associations, individual bosses and the players themselves.

As the BBC reported in 2013: "There is understandable frustration…in the lesbian, gay, bisexual and transgender (LGBT) community that football is dragging its heels. They are fast learning that the gears in football grind at a much slower pace off the pitch than the football played on it."

As a result of all this, conventional wisdom was that a large-scale campaign against homophobia in football was unlikely to take off at the present time.

A FRESH STRATEGIC APPROACH: MISSION AND MISCHIEF

It was obvious that Paddy Power would have to do something different to succeed where so many others had failed. Recognising the scale of the task, it invited Stonewall to join with it so that it could tap into the group's experience in this area.

In some ways it was an unlikely combination: Paddy Power is often described as the *enfant terrible* of marketing, while Stonewall, like any charity, has an intrinsically serious purpose. However, this apparent mismatch is precisely what made this partnership so powerful.

The partners defined their joint strategy as a mixture of "mission and mischief." Stonewall obviously had lots of experience when it came to the former, while Paddy Power could supply plenty of the latter. Both elements were crucial and complementary: too much "mission" and people would dismiss the campaign as worthy (as they had done other initiatives in this field), while too much "mischief" and the public would complain of trivialisation.

Specifically, they set themselves three objectives:
- Get people talking about this taboo.
- Generate and show mass support for gay footballers.
- Do this in a way that was true to both partners' brands.

Equally crucially, they were determined to avoid three things which would undermine the cause:
- They actively didn't want to "out" players.
- Or pressurise people to give support.
- Or seek a direct financial return.

A BIG CREATIVE IDEA: LIKE A RAINBOW

This strategic balancing act was dramatised in one big idea. Send rainbow-coloured bootlaces to every professional football club in the land and ask players to wear them in their next match. Some deliberately provocative language was used to get people talking with the strapline "Right Behind Gay Footballers" (Figures 1 and 2).

Advertising legend Sir John Hegarty named the idea his pick of the year, calling it "Brilliantly simple…everyone wins…I love it."*Creative Review* also named it one of the top campaigns of 2013, while BuzzFeed called it "Brilliant" and Thinkbox described it as "Great stuff!".

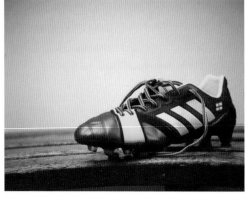

Figure 1. The big idea

Figure 2. Getting people talking

A POWERFUL ACTIVATION CAMPAIGN

A potent mix of advertising, PR, digital and social media were now used to amplify this big idea and generate as much public support as possible. To make the most of the limited (£150,000) funds, activity was focused on just one week in September. In particular, media partnerships were formed with *Metro*, Twitter and talkSPORT, with meetings held twice a day to adjust the messaging to ensure that the campaign was kept high on the news agenda.

- For the first few days the campaign's aim was just about establishing the idea.
- Then midweek, criticism from some clubs had to be addressed. They complained that they hadn't been given enough warning but this had been anticipated: the surprise tactics were a deliberate ploy to ensure that bureaucracy did not neuter the campaign. The organisers knew that the public would see these complaints as "pathetic…eerily similar…almost as if centrally controlled." So all that had to be done was to poke fun at the lack of logic and empower players to take action (Figure 3).
- Later in the week, the focus turned to the big Manchester derby, and one last push. Then on the Monday afterwards, everybody involved was thanked for their extraordinary support.

In addition to these key media partnerships, footballer Joey Barton was picked as an ambassador for their cause. As with all the celebrities who supported the campaign, he didn't receive a penny, but he was a particularly strong advocate given his huge social following and strong personal belief (Figure 4).

Figure 3. Activation campaign

Figure 4. Joey Barton as advocate

CHANGING THE RULES OF THE GAME

The campaign more than met its three objectives.

1. Getting people to talk about this taboo

- The campaign attracted over 400 media stories, with a combined reach of over 500 million. These included 35 pieces of TV coverage, 161 radio items and 250 print/online stories (Figure 5).
- Meanwhile, another 320 million impressions were generated on Twitter. Paddy Power's launch tweet received over 2,200 retweets (20 times the norm) and the brand picked up 3,600 new followers in the process.
- Social engagement levels rose by 74% in five days and, by the end of the week, the #RBGF hashtag had received 72,000 mentions. In fact, the hashtag trended worldwide, organically, not once, but twice that week.

Figure 5. The word spreads

In the words of one media blog, the campaign "seemed to appear overnight but then suddenly it was everywhere."

2. Generating support for gay footballers

Players from 54 professional clubs wore the laces (Figure 6), from Arsenal to Aberdeen, Everton to East Fife. Big name managers like Arsène Wenger were also vocal in their support and Newcastle boss Alan Pardew even wore some rainbow laces on the touchline. Famous ex-pros like Stan Collymore, Matt Le Tissier and John Hartson chimed in. Gary Lineker wore laces on *Match of the Day*, David Ginola showed his off on *BT Sport*, while Max Rushden donned his on *Soccer AM*.

Figure 6. Support grows

After years of silence, it seemed like everybody in the game was making up for lost time. But, crucially, the campaign soon began to spread far beyond football. A host of celebrities tweeted their support, from Stephen Fry to Boy George, Claire Balding to Matt Lucas, Ed Miliband to Ed Balls. The Scottish Parliament passed a motion in favour of the campaign, the Department of Culture and Sport did likewise and MPs even sported rainbow laces in their annual kickabout.

Other sports joined in. Rugby players at Wasps wore the laces, while legendary figures from tennis (Boris Becker and Martina Navratilova), racing (Ruby Walsh) and boxing (Ricky Hatton) tweeted support for their footballing peers. By the end of the week, even other brands were getting 'Right Behind Gay Footballers' – most notably Umbro, Aviva and Dr Martens.

Perhaps most significantly, thousands of fans got involved to the extent that another 10,000 sets of laces had to be produced to try and meet public demand.

In the words of the independent Gay Footballers' Supporters' Network (GFSN): "We are thrilled by the outpouring of support for LGBT footballers…it's really captured the imagination of the public…this campaign is a watershed moment."

3. Being true to both partners' brands
At the end of the week, David Wilding of PHD wrote that "The respective strengths of the brands make this the perfect collaboration. It has been a highly impressive

effort, with each part gaining more energy from one another." This subjective view was borne out by quantitative research by YouGov. Encouragingly for Paddy Power, 43% of regular betters were aware of the campaign, and of these 47% thought better of Paddy Power as a result (versus only 4% who thought worse).

Equally positively for Stonewall, Google analysis shows that four months after the activity all top 10 search results for "Gay footballers UK campaign" mentioned the charity (with nine of them specifically referring to rainbow laces), and none of them mentioning other initiatives.

AN EFFECTIVE RETURN ON INVESTMENT

This activity was explicitly *not* designed to generate a profit. But, for the organisers, it was definitely money well spent in several ways.

- The value of the free editorial coverage. This is notoriously hard to quantify, but the value of 500 million media impacts and 320 million Twitter impressions was much higher than the cost of the £150,000 campaign.
- Secondly, there was the impact on brand equity. A quantitative survey showed that over 687,000 regular betters (nearly half of the core audience) were more favourable towards Paddy Power with respective increased purchase intent as a result of the campaign.
- Lastly, but most importantly, has been the societal impact. While this is hard to measure, the evidence comes from the millions of people who saw and talked about a previously taboo issue, the tens of thousands who actively supported the campaign, wore the laces, and joined Paddy Power and Stonewall on social media, and the countless individuals who wrote to thank them.

To put this into context, the campaign cost less than 1% of its annual budget, less than 0.2% of category spend and less than half of Wayne Rooney's weekly pay!

All images appearing in this case study are reproduced by permission of Paddy Power.

THE DEPAUL BOX COMPANY
Thinking outside the box

SNAPSHOT

A small charity which helps young homeless people get off the street combined a tiny budget with a big idea to create a sustainable source of funds for its work.

AGENCY

Publicis London

KEY INSIGHTS

- Depaul UK needed to overcome the challenge of donor fatigue without the financial resources of its much bigger charitable counterparts.
- Research brought two valuable insights: people are adept at shielding themselves from guilt when they see the homeless while at the same time they most appreciate the idea of having a home when moving – and moving means boxes.
- Spending just £7,500 to set up a commercial venture to sell boxes gave the charity a permanent source of funds to meet its target of doubling the beds available by 2016.

SUMMARY

Depaul UK is a charity that helps young homeless people get off the street before it's too late. At the beginning of 2012 the charity put in place an ambitious objective to double the number of bed nights it could offer by 2016 since demand for its services was outstripping supply.

However, research confirmed that a traditional advertising campaign was not only well beyond its resources but wouldn't be that effective in such a crowded market, so exploration began to find an alternative method for fundraising. House movers were found to be an interesting segment since they have the potential to be empathetic with the cause as they're experiencing (in a very different way) a similar sort of upheaval to those without a home.

Lateral thinking led to the founding of the Depaul Box Company with an initial investment of just £7,500 to sell cardboard boxes to move belongings to a new home, with all profits helping the homeless move off the streets. It partnered with a manufacturer to produce suitable boxes which also carried printed stories of those the charity had helped.

To save on promotional costs, Depaul worked with an e-commerce platform provider which offered a level of customisation, data capture and social media opportunities, while also mounting a press and outdoor awareness campaign. By the end of 2013 more than 15,000 boxes had been sold.

IT'S COLD OUT THERE

Depaul UK is a charity that helps young people who are homeless get off the street before it's too late. 80,000 young people experience homelessness each year, often through no fault of their own. The choices facing a young person on the street are stark. They're cold, they're lonely and they're despondent. It's no surprise that three in four young people who spend more than one night on the street end up taking hard drugs (Figure 1).

Figure 1. Sleeping rough

In the face of this, Depaul UK provides frontline services for young homeless people nationwide. That includes literally picking people up off the street at the moment when they are most vulnerable and finding them secure accommodation at a moment's notice.

In 2013, figures suggested that there were 23% more people sleeping rough than three years ago, with a disproportionate number of them aged 16-25 (Figure 2). In this context, demand for Depaul UK services was seriously outpacing supply, so the charity set in place the ambitious goal of doubling the amount of bed nights that it could offer to young homeless people by 2016. It then began to explore fundraising strategies to meet this challenging objective.

Figure 2. The stark truth

A CROWDED MARKET

There has long been a traditional approach for charity advertising. You restate the problem and remind people of the injustice, ensuring you chip away at their conscience along the way, before asking them to help solve the problem by making a contribution. Essentially it boils down to two things: engineering sympathy and appealing for generosity (Figure 3).

For a small charity like Depaul UK, this approach brings with it a number of problems. The main one is that too many charities are asking too many of the same people to care about their issue above all others, without being able to explain why their good cause is any more worthy than the rest. It's hard to stand out from the other 163,153 charities trying to raise money.

To make matters worse, the scale of the competition is particularly daunting. The top ten charities in the UK spent an average of £11 million each on advertising alone in 2012. But the sheer quantity of charity communications has had a

Figure 3. Charity adverts

much more profound effect too. These sympathy tactics have resulted in an audience conditioned to shield off any 'guilt trip' attempts on sight in an effort to protect their own personal well being.

Depaul wanted to prove that this 'shield' existed, but felt sure that conventional research wouldn't yield results. After all, who would publicly admit in a focus group that they often ignore someone poor and disadvantaged out on the street? To confirm the existence of this shield, it needed to carry out a field experiment.

GATHERING INSIGHTS

Depaul sent people out onto the streets clad in suitable attire that made them look like rough sleepers. On two afternoons in central London they pitched a spot outside the workplaces of friends and past colleagues. It was a successful afternoon. But it was also a painful one. (And not just because they only collected a dismal 27p.)

It was deeply uncomfortable watching their own friends and colleagues actively turning their heads to avoid pangs of guilt, unwittingly walking right past people they've spent many happy days and nights with (Figure 4a,4b,4c). The charity's suspicions were correct: if the sight of homeless people on the street, cold, tired and hungry, made people raise their 'sympathy shield', then an ad wasn't going to help all that much either.

Figure 4a. Walking on by   Figure 4b.   Figure 4c.

This led to the first useful consumer insight: the majority of the charity's audience was adept at shielding themselves from any 'guilt trip' attempts (including advertising) on sight. Raising money by getting people to care made perfect sense in theory, but in practice, most charities only succeed in making a marginal improvement.

The challenge was that Depaul UK's growth strategy simply wouldn't be possible with a marginal improvement. To double the number of bed nights by 2016, it would have to change the way it financed its operations permanently.

After much thought, the charity realised that its best plan would be to speak to people when that shield is lowered – perhaps when the audience felt a natural link with its cause. It believed there existed a higher emotional ground to sympathy and that it should instead speak to people during moments of empathy. That would help shift the audience from a position on the outside, looking in, to a position where they might have an appreciation of what a homeless person is going through.

That led to the beginning of an exploration of times at which an audience might feel empathetic with homeless people. It seemed sensible to conclude that those times would correlate with points throughout their life at which the value of home became much more prominent. Research through focus groups showed the increased value that is placed upon home after extended business trips, or during family birthdays and the Christmas period.

But there was one life-stage that the participants seemed altogether more animated about during discussion and when the value of home stood out most of all: moving house. Key findings were:

- Your home is your shelter in every way imaginable.
- And when you move house everything becomes chaotic.
- For a little moment, you feel displaced.
- For a short space of time, your shelter is gone.
- Home movers are experiencing (in a microcosmic way) the feeling of upheaval that young homeless people experience every single day.

This led to the second guiding insight: people most understand the value of home when they are in the process of moving home

SEARCHING FOR A NEW MODEL
Depaul could have used those insights to mount an ad campaign aimed at those moving households. The potential audience figures were certainly large enough: 3.8 million households had either moved in the last 12 months, or were planning to do so in the next 12 months. In addition, one in seven households move every two years (Figure 5).

Length of residence in current home by tenure, 2010-11

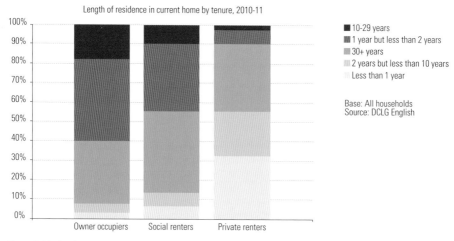

Figure 5. Moving house

However, further analysis showed that a home-moving state of mind didn't prove particularly conducive to ad effectiveness. House movers were so wrapped up in all the administration, legal issues, tidying and packing up that they didn't have the capacity to take time out to donate to charities. Despite that feeling of empathy, appealing for generosity simply wouldn't work.

After much thought, Depaul worked out that the only way they would take time to help the cause was if the charity could help them in some way. So it stopped seeking donations and started searching for a way to offer some sort of utility instead.

This inspired the thought of the dual role cardboard boxes can play. People associate cardboard boxes with homeless people. When winter draws in and there's no place else to go, it's the cardboard box that helps to protect a young homeless person from the elements. And it is cardboard boxes that home movers need to transport things from one home to the next (Figure 6).

That led to the founding of the Depaul Box Company to sell cardboard boxes to people who are moving house. They are just like other boxes.

Figure 6. Making the move

In other words, a parity product in a highly commoditised marketplace, except for one big difference: all of the profit goes to helping young homeless people. This was about asking people to buy something that they would need in order to move house and presenting them with a way to help a homeless person out at the same time.

Founding the company (and the initial investment in box stock) cost £7,500 in total. The production of subsequent box stock was funded using the profits of the first batch.

BIRTH OF A BUSINESS

A brand-by-brand analysis of the strengths/weaknesses/opportunities/threats (SWOT) in the current market made it clear that there was little differentiation. Competitors were all selling parity products:

- Small, medium and large packs of boxes with two to four different sizes of box.
- A mix of single- and double-walled boxes to ensure adequate strength given the likely load for the different sizes of box.
- A free pen and tape to help with assembling and labelling the boxes.
- A non-specific commitment to using recycled pulp in the manufacturing process, with nobody able to ensure that 100% of source material was recycled.
- Sold online with free delivery anywhere in the UK.

Pricing analysis showed clear price point clusters around box packs too (Figure 7). Depaul's aim was to ensure that its boxes were completely undifferentiated in

Box sales – price analysis clusters

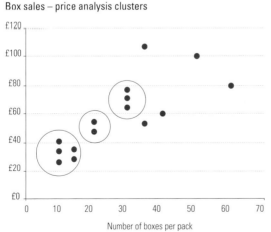

Figure 7. Pricing analysis

almost every way except for one major element: it would be the only product in the marketplace which would donate 100% of the profits to helping young homeless people.

Manufacturing
In terms of manufacturing, the company needed a partner who could manufacture boxes that not only matched the specifications of anything else in the market, but also carried stories about young homeless people who have been helped by Depaul UK. After months of searching, the charity found a box company that could deliver exactly what it wanted and ordered its first batch of 2000 boxes (Figure 8a, 8b, 8c, 8d).

Figure 8a. Making the boxes

Figure 8b. Making the boxes

Figure 8c. Making the boxes

Figure 8d. The finished product

Sales channels
Depaul worked with an existing e-commerce platform provider to ensure expenditure was kept to a minimum. A certain level of customisation was available to create a branded experience, and the website enabled sharing to social platforms and data capture of customers to build the Depaul UK database.

Communications

Establishing a working business model was followed by building a working communications model. It began with the boxes themselves, which were a great canvas for telling a story about a young homeless person helped by Depaul UK. Positioning images and stories of a young homeless person not only made the person using the box feel good, but it ensured that all of their new neighbours knew that they were a good person too.

A press and outdoor campaign raised awareness of the Depaul Box Company, and the strength of the idea enabled the business to pitch successfully for free media from media owners with unfilled bookings at the time of launch. The PR and social media campaign was built on the notion that the Depaul Box Company was a totally new way of raising money for charity to ensure that as many people as possible knew about what was happening. Key opinion formers were also encouraged to talk about the Depaul Box Company (Figures 9 and 10).

Figure 9. Promoting the business

Figure 10. Spreading the word

The Depaul UK Trading CIC became a legal entity on 13th March 2013, and the Depaul Box Company began shipping boxes to house movers straight away. By the end of the year 15,000 boxes had been sold, while the company also moved to much larger warehouse premises. Ambitious plans were put in place that included a new communications plan, potential partnerships with estate agents, a tie-in with a property website and the exploration of other sales channels.

All images appearing in this case study are reproduced by permission of Depaul UK.

APPENDIX

The case studies in this book have won, been highly commended or finalists for the following Marketing Society awards. The names of the original agencies involved (where applicable) are also included.

Organisation	Category	Year
AMVBBDO	Employee engagement	2014
Aviva *Agency: Teamspirit*	B2B	2013
Axe (Unilever) *Agency: Bartle Bogle Hegarty*	Global marketing	2013
British Airways *Agency: Bartle Bogle Hegarty*	Brand revitalisation	2013
British Gas *Agency: CHI & Partners, Carat*	Marketing for sustainable consumption	2014
BT Sport *Agency: AMVBBDO*	Brand extension Brand revitalisation	2014
Burton's Biscuit Company	Marketing leadership	2014
The Depaul Box Company *Agency: Publicis London*	Marketing on a shoestring Not-for-profit marketing Best leading-edge thinking	2014

easyJet *Agencies: VCCP, OMD UK,* *Havas EHS*	Grand prix Finance directors' prize Long-term marketing excellence Customer relationship marketing E-commerce	2014
The Fairtrade Foundation	Marketing for sustainable consumption	2013
The Famous Grouse *Agency: The BIG Partnership*	Global marketing	2012
Foster's *Agency: adam&eveDDB*	Long-term marketing excellence	2014
Hailo *Agency: Rothco*	New brand	2014
Jack Daniel's Tennessee Honey	Brand extension	2014
Jaguar F-Type *Agencies: Spark44, Mindshare,* *Brooklyn Brothers*	Brand revitalisation, Brand extension	2014
John Lewis *Agencies: adam&eveDDB,* *Manning Gottlieb OMD*	Long-term marketing excellence Brand activation Marketing communications	2013/2014
Macmillan Cancer Support *Agency: VCCP*	Customer insight Not-for-profit marketing	2014
Mars Galaxy *Agency: AMVBBDO*	Marketing communications	2014
McDonald's *Agencies: Leo Burnett, OMD,* *The Marketing Store*	Marketing communications	2013

McLaren *Agency: VCCP London*	Brand extension	2013
Mercedes-Benz *Agencies: AMVBBDO, Maxus,* *Weapon7, Holler*	Customer insight	2014
MINI *Agency: iris*	Social media marketing	2014
National Lottery *Agency: AMVBBDO*	Brand revitalisation	2014
Notcutts Garden Centre Group *Agencies: babyGRAND* *Marketing, Coniak*	Customer relationship marketing Finance director's prize	2013
Paddy Power *Agencies: Crispin Porter &* *Bogusky, M2M, Lucky Generals*	Cause-related marketing Brand activation Marketing communications	2013/4
PwC *Agency: Civilian*	Marketing for sustainable consumption	2014
Sainsbury's Christmas *Agencies: AMVBBDO, PHD,* *Blue Rubicon*	Content marketing Social media marketing	2014
Sainsbury's/Channel 4 Paralympics *Agency: AMVBBDO*	Grand Prix Cause-related marketing	2013
Telefonica O_2 Priority Moments *Agency: Cherry London*	Mobile marketing	2013
Unilever small cans *Agencies: Lowe Group,* *Clarion Communications*	Marketing for sustainable consumption	2014

INDEX